A Handbook of Research on Global Peace Governance and the Sustainable Development of Economies

A Handbook of Research on Global Peace Governance and the Sustainable Development of Economies

By

Unmana Sarangi

Cambridge
Scholars
Publishing

A Handbook of Research on Global Peace Governance
and the Sustainable Development of Economies

By Unmana Sarangi

This book first published 2023

Cambridge Scholars Publishing

Lady Stephenson Library, Newcastle upon Tyne, NE6 2PA, UK

British Library Cataloguing in Publication Data
A catalogue record for this book is available from the British Library

ISBN (10): 1-5275-2944-4
ISBN (13): 978-1-5275-2944-1

TABLE OF CONTENTS

ABSTRACT

The research study entitled **"Global Peace, Governance and the Sustainable Development of Economies"** focuses on detailing the aspects of global peace, governance issues and analyzes the global economic systems and the various international organizations that work in coordination with the other national and international organizations, civil societies, NGOs to attain peace, justice and effective global governance, to achieve SDGs and sustainable development slated by the UN by the turn of 2030. It also studies the various issues pertaining to developing new economic partnerships for SDGs and the role of private multilateral international institutions in effective implementation of the SDGs of the UN through a proper and effective coordination and working in synergy with these institutions with the UN on the one hand and the other related national and international institutions such as other private multilateral institutions, NGOs, civil societies, world class academic institutions on the other to attain peace, governance, justice and SDGs. The aspect-wise review of literature i.e. global peace, governance, justice and SDGs has been reflected in brief studied by various authors. The functions of the various international organizations such as IMF, World Bank and WTO etc., in providing financial assistance and in developing rules and frameworks to achieve these objectives have also been studied. The role and functions of the United Nations with regards to promotion of new global partnerships, peace, and governance including the role of private international organizations and multiregional trade complexes have also been highlighted. It is observed that the purpose of these international institutions which were created, were primarily to provide financing to the developing organizations including framing of rules and procedures for effective and harmonious global economic development. However, the tilt is towards giving more attention to developed economies and the focus on developing economies has been minimal. This has jeopardized the growth and development of these developing economies and reduced their participation and stakeholder ship in the global forum/international community to attain effective and proper global economic development. This has posed a serious challenge to attain global peace, effective global governance and in turn promotion of SDGs. Hence, it would be appropriate and in the fitness of things to confer adequate and proper autonomy to these national institutions of importance working in various developing economies/countries to carve a niche for themselves to participate in adequate representations to make the international/global agenda as slated by the UN, effective and successful. This in turn would definitely go a long way in attaining global peace, governance and justice and in achieving the SDGs by turn of 2030 as adopted by the United Nations.

Key Words: Global Peace, Governance, Justice, the UN Agenda, SDGs, Private Multilateral Institutions, Multiregional trade complexes

INTRODUCTION

TRANSFORMING OUR WORLD: THE 2030 AGENDA FOR SUSTAINABLE DEVELOPMENT

The 2030 Agenda for Sustainable Development makes an unequivocal call to change the way partnerships have been done in the past to transcend institutional and sectoral divisions and create innovative forms of cooperation among governments, civil society, and the private sector. Making peace is often thought of as a task for states and their multilateral partners. But while governments have a central role to play in building a more peaceful world, businesses and civil society organizations can do more to support and scale up such efforts. By acknowledging the role of the private sector as a partner in sustainable development and simultaneously connecting sustainable development with peace, the 2030 Agenda provides a tangible link between the private sector and peace. As such, it can serve as an entry point for the business community to contribute to building and sustaining peaceful societies.

This joint research project by the SDG Fund, Concordia, and the International Peace Institute focuses on the following questions: (i) What does it mean in practice for the private sector to become a partner for sustainable development and sustaining peace; (ii) How can companies reduce the risks associated with investing in countries under stress; and (iii) what are the tools to scale up investments and unlock the resources needed to implement the 2030 Agenda. To answer these questions, each institution brought to the table its own particular experience and expertise. As a multi-donor and multi-agency mechanism, the SDG Fund brought its experience engaging the private sector as a partner in more than twenty-two countries and the lessons learned from this collaboration. Concordia, as a global platform and incubator for partnerships, leveraged its community to uncover private-sector-driven approaches to engaging with the Sustainable Development Goals (SDGs). As an independent, research-based think tank with extensive experience working with the UN and its member states, the International Peace Institute provided access to UN officials and agencies and led the research and editorial process. The report also seeks to contribute to ongoing discussions on the repositioning of the UN development system to deliver on the 2030 Agenda. Forging a strong and effective global partnership between the public and private sectors would be pivotal in determining the fate of the SDGs and building a more peaceful and inclusive world.

To meet the scale and ambition of the 2030 Agenda for Sustainable Development, the private sector will have to play a central role. The agenda provides a window of opportunity for the private sector, governments, and the UN to collaborate with each other through a new global partnership. To make this partnership a reality, the UN and its member states must take steps to build trust with the private sector, including with small and medium enterprises, by engaging with it through a more systematic, transparent, and inclusive approach. The private sector, for its part, needs to transform itself into a partner by embedding the Sustainable Development Goals (SDGs) directly into its core business strategies and reporting on its contributions to achieving them, motivated by an advanced understanding of profit.

The private sector also needs to recognize the role it can play in building and sustaining peace. In the 2030 Agenda, peace is not only a goal in itself (SDG 16) but also a cross-cutting theme that drives the achievement of the agenda as a whole. SDG 5 on gender equality, SDG 8 on inclusive economic growth, and SDG 17 on global partnership, in particular, are among the relevant goals that provide entry points for the private sector to engage in promoting peace.

The 2030 Agenda can therefore help bridge the current gap between the private sector and peace, promoting a holistic vision of peace where the private sector has a role. By adopting a “sustaining peace” approach, businesses can support the strengthening of effective, inclusive, and accountable institutions, build trust with communities, and empower youth and women as central actors in development and peace.

In order to bridge this gap, there is a need for more businesses to invest and create partnerships in countries they typically see as too risky. This requires exploring innovative tools to incentivize investment by reducing risk. Such tools, including blended finance, pooling mechanisms, micro finance, and development impact bonds, present further opportunities for partnership between the public and private sectors and the UN.

CHAPTER I

RECOMMENDATIONS TO CREATE A NEW PARTNERSHIP FOR THE SDGS

In order to bridge the gap between the private sector and peace, and incentivize private investment in countries under stress the following are the recommendations of the joint research project of the SDG Fund viz;

(i) Businesses should embed the SDGs in their core business strategies by integrating them in supply chains, practices and policies.

(ii) Businesses should improve reporting on their contributions to the SDGs, including by working with the UN to connect the SDG targets with business performance indicators.

(iii) Businesses should expand engagement with UN headquarters through the high-level political forum and UN General Assembly summits on the follow-up and review of the 2030 Agenda.

(iv) Global leaders should emphasize that the SDGs are good for business, better communicating to businesses that the SDGs represent an economic opportunity.

(v) The UN, governments, and large companies should increase engagement with small and medium enterprises, which should play a bigger role in efforts to achieve the SDGs.

(vi) Governments and businesses should work together more closely in implementing the SDGs, with businesses supporting national governments in strengthening public institutions.

(vii) Businesses should take a sustaining peace approach to their operations, assessing not only how their work can avoid contributing to conflict but also how it can support efforts to build and sustain peace.

(viii) Businesses should build trust with communities by establishing open and transparent communication channels, setting up clear expectations, and providing space for community members to express their grievances and priorities.

(ix) Businesses should strive to be more inclusive, including by adopting more inclusive hiring practices and targeting youth and women as the main beneficiaries of their operations.

(x) The UN, governments, and businesses should partner to scale up investments in countries under stress, including through mechanisms such as blended finance, pooling mechanisms, and development impact bonds.

(xi) The new partnership between governments, the UN, and businesses should not focus on one-off programs. Projects require long-term, self-sustaining funding models and a wider diversity of investors.

(xii) The 2030 Agenda for Sustainable Development makes a bold and determined promise: "To transform our world" and "to reach the furthest behind first." It commits to end poverty in all its forms, address climate change, and promote peaceful and inclusive societies. To achieve these goals, it calls for a new global partnership built through inclusive alliances between governments, businesses, civil society organizations, and the UN system.

(xiii) The role of the private sector is prominent throughout the 2030 Agenda, most notably in Sustainable Development Goal (SDG) 17, which highlights the need to "strengthen the means of implementation and revitalize the Global Partnership for Sustainable Development." The agenda explicitly calls on businesses "to apply their creativity and innovation to solving sustainable development challenges." The call is directed to the private sector in all its forms, "from micro-enterprises to cooperatives to multinationals," recognizing that the private sector is not monolithic but highly diverse in scale and capacity.

This call is also echoed in the 2015 Addis Ababa Action Agenda, a framework for intergovernmental financing for development that provides concrete measures private investors can take to align themselves with sustainable development. Similarly, the resolutions on "sustaining peace," adopted by the UN General Assembly and Security Council in 2016, call for a new strategic partnership with the private sector to promote inclusive growth and foster peaceful societies. The first goal is to explore what is needed to forge a new, holistic partnership between businesses, the UN, and its member states to achieve the 2030 Agenda, as called for in the agenda itself. The 2030 Agenda has opened a window of opportunity for building this partnership, and there are promising signs that progress toward enduring cross-sector collaborations are already underway. The research study covers both the private sector and the UN who have agreed that the 2030 Agenda has provided a new space to build trust and bridge gaps. The UN Secretary-General and the CEOs of several major multinational companies have already expressed their commitment to turning the vision of the 2030 Agenda into reality. UN Secretary-General has reiterated and shown interest in the "alignment of the core business of the private sector with the strategic goals of the international community," envisioning a "new generation of partnerships with the business community".

(xiv) However, this window of opportunity will not be open forever, and changes are still required from the UN, member states, and the private sector to take advantage of it. Many businesses mentioned that the UN and its member states must take steps to build trust with the private sector, including small and medium enterprises (SMEs), by engaging with it through a more systematic, transparent, and inclusive approach. For its part, the private sector needs to transform itself into a partner by embedding the SDGs directly into its core business strategies and reporting on its contributions to achieving them. This is the equivalent of incorporating the 2030 Agenda into businesses' DNA.

(xv) By changing their behavior, culture, structure and embedding the SDGs in their supply chains and bottom-line metrics. These changes need to come from the top: "The leadership has to prove the business case for engaging in the SDGs."

The second goal is to understand how the private sector in all its forms from large companies and investors to SMEs can contribute to achieving peace as both an enabler and an outcome of the 2030 Agenda, including through SDG 5, SDG 8, SDG 16 and SDG 17. This requires businesses to adopt a "sustaining peace" approach to all their operations and investments. Sustaining peace is defined by member states as "A goal and a process to build a common vision of a society, ensuring that the needs of all segments of the population are taken into account, which encompasses activities aimed at preventing the outbreak, escalation, continuation and recurrence of conflict, addressing root causes, assisting parties to conflict to end hostilities, ensuring national reconciliation, and moving towards recovery, reconstruction and development".

For the private sector, adopting a sustaining peace approach requires building trust-based relationships with national and local governments and engaging with local communities during decision making. This is not a "one-size-fits-all" approach but requires an understanding and awareness of the specific context.

Like the 2030 Agenda, which states that "there can be no sustainable development without peace and no peace without sustainable development," this study understands peace in a holistic manner. The 2030 Agenda portrays peace not only as a goal in itself, but also SDG 16 calls for the promotion of peaceful, just, and inclusive societies and as a cross-cutting theme that drives the achievement of the agenda as a whole. As opined by a CEO of a major multinational company, "The bottom line is that peace and development are a prerequisite for each other."

This represents a powerful shift in mindset toward conceiving of peace in an active and "positive" way from looking at the factors that drive violent conflict to those that enable and sustain peace. This is particularly important when addressing the role of the private sector in promoting peace, as many companies do not see themselves as "peace actors." When peace is portrayed as a continuum that requires progress in all aspects of sustainable development, the role of the private sector in promoting peace becomes clearer.

Although businesses have an impact on all of the SDGs, and all of them are linked to peace, the research study pays particular attention to four SDGs through which the private sector can make a particularly strong contribution to peace: SDG 5 on gender equality, SDG 8 on inclusive economic growth, SDG 16 on peaceful and just societies, and SDG 17 on a new global partnership. These four SDGs connect directly to the role of business in sustaining peace.

For instance, "a universal, rules-based, open, non-discriminatory and equitable trading system" (SDG 17) can, with the right policies in place, be an engine of inclusive economic growth. This could in turn contribute to increasing employment (SDG 8 and women's inclusion (SDG 5), which has a direct effect on a state's level of peacefulness (SDG 16), as gender equality is a strong predictor of peace.

In forging new partnerships around sustainable development and sustaining peace, the UN, member states, and the private sector need to change their mindsets and behaviors to place the needs of people at the center of their approach. This is particularly true in countries that are under stress, whether they are developed or developing countries, free from conflict or affected by conflict. This broad category of "countries under stress" includes those that need to strengthen governance and public institutions and pose a higher degree of risk for both domestic and foreign companies. The World Bank has a similar term: "low-income countries under stress." However, since many middle-income countries also experience high levels of poverty and governance deficits, the term used here encompasses a broader spectrum of countries. Enhancing the private sector's involvement and increasing investment in the SDGs in these complex contexts that often lack investment can have a major impact on the lives of millions of people. The third goal therefore, is to address the most pressing concern that companies have about investing and commencing operations in countries under stress: how can their risk be mitigated. According to the UN Secretary-General, "In spite of an increasingly conducive environment, SDGs investments continue to lack scale. Cross-sectoral partnerships and a blending of capital are also proving complex for many governments. To date, the lack of 'bankable' projects has been a major impediment to greater SDG investment." To address this, the study analyzes how several financial instruments can be used to cushion companies from the risks associated with working with and in countries under stress and to scale up projects in those countries. According to the UN Secretary-General, to achieve the 2030 Agenda "governments will need more support to attract, leverage and mobilize investments of all kinds public and private, national and global." Crafting inclusive partnerships with the private sector is essential to delivering on and transforming the promise of this agenda into reality. But at the same time, the private sector cannot be expected to be the only solution to sustainable development, let alone peace. Moreover, many companies reiterated that there is a need to manage expectations; this is "a new journey" that requires time and adjustment. The SDGs should not be used to repackage existing practices or to clean up the image of human rights abusers and should not be "cherry-picked" as convenient. Therefore, partnerships with the private sector need to be built on transparency and mutual accountability.

Research of IPI and Concordia

The research conducted by IPI and Concordia are based on interviews and questionnaires with large corporations with a global footprint that are working on the SDGs in a range of sectors. IPI also interviewed many UN agencies and civil society organizations that work alongside the private sector toward achieving the 2030 Agenda. This research study also draws on the portfolio of the SDG Fund to reflect on the lessons learned from international and local companies working in countries under stress.

Creating a New Global Partnership

There is a need to forge a new, holistic partnership between businesses, the UN, and its member states to achieve the 2030 Agenda. Changes are still required from all sides to deepen this partnership and build trust.

Deepening UN Engagement with the Private Sector

Companies perceive that there has been a change in the way the UN and member states engage with the private sector. There is a new wave of openness and a greater recognition of the role businesses play in contributing to sustainable development and peace. Now there is a collaborative approach, with the UN and member states acknowledging that the private sector and private finance are needed and willing to help them achieve the SDGs.

The SDG Fund, a multi-donor, multi-agency UN mechanism, is at the center of this emerging collaborative approach. In 2015 the SDG Fund launched a Private Sector Advisory Group (PSAG) composed of business leaders of major companies from various industries worldwide. There is a growing enthusiasm among multilateral institutions for greater involvement of businesses. Earlier there was a difference in understanding between governments, businesses and civil society. There is a felt need of the private sector to play its role in SDG Fund mechanisms for attaining inclusive economic growth, peaceful and sustainable societies. The 2030 Agenda helped instigate this conversation by providing a common framework that recognizes the different but complementary roles of business and the UN in achieving peace and sustainable development. In line with the 2030 Agenda's understanding of the SDGs as holistic and inter-linked, the SDG Fund is undertaking projects that work with the private sector as a co-designer and partner to address multiple SDGs and focus on transforming the entire production system, in order to sell the final product. The SDG Fund works with the support of a Secretariat based in New York to help UN country teams identify private sector partners. After going through a due-diligence process, representatives from the government, the private sector, and the UN co-design and co-invest in a project that is context-specific and that promotes multiple SDGs. The SDG Fund emphasizes the idea of investing in projects that can unlock market-wide benefits and that can be sustainable and replicated. A clear example of this partnership is the SDG Fund's joint program in Nigeria, which is not only training a group of young farmers to help them overcome poverty but also attempting to alleviate poverty on a wider scale by strengthening the agro-food value chains. This type of collaboration is not new, but historically the private sector was primarily seen as a donor. Long before the 2030 Agenda, the UN system engaged the private sector in different ways some more visible than others and this engagement extends beyond development. Most UN agencies and inter-governmental bodies have methods for engaging the private sector in policy making. The 2030 Agenda helped in providing a common framework that recognizes the different but complementary roles of businesses and the UN in achieving peace and sustainable development. In line with the 2030 Agenda's understanding of the SDGs as holistic and inter-linked, the SDG Fund is undertaking projects that work with the private sector as a co-designer and partner to address multiple SDGs and focus on transforming the entire production system, from planting the seeds to selling the final product.

Tackling multiple SDGs by using a market-wide approach in Nigeria

The SDG Funds "Food Africa" project in Nigeria reflects the new type of global partnership envisaged in the 2030 Agenda, it tackles multiple SDGs through a market-wide approach, engages the private sector as a co-designer, strengthens the role of the UN resident coordinators' office as a platform to connect the national government, the local private sector, and UN agencies, and, most importantly, puts people at the center of its programming. This public-private partnership brings together the energy conglomerate Sahara Group, the SDG Fund, the UN offices in Nigeria, the "Roca Brothers" chefs, and the Kaduna state government in Nigeria. It aims at improving food security and alleviating poverty using a market-driven model for agricultural development that strengthens agro-food value chains, improves agricultural productivity and yields, enhances food-processing facilities, and promotes access to markets in Nigeria. The

SDG Fund and Sahara Group work together in designing the program and provide the bulk of the co-financing, mobilizing matching contributions, and overseeing the preparation and implementation of the work plan in agreement with the other partners. The office of the UN resident coordinator in Nigeria coordinates with relevant UN agencies, FAO, ILO and ITC. These provide technical assistance in their areas of expertise to implement the activities agreed upon in the work plan. Using a training-of-trainers model, the Roca Brothers, internationally acclaimed chefs, mentor a select group of market horticultural products and share best practices in using a training-of-trainers model, the Roca Brothers, internationally acclaimed chefs, mentor a select group of farmers in cultivating, processing and bringing to market horticultural products and share best practices in using resources efficiently, recycling and recovering waste. The Kaduna state government provides the arable land, the facility, utilities and year-round security. Further, the state government collaborates with other state-level stakeholders to improve local infrastructure farmland, share relevant policy information and data, and identify farmers to take part in the programme encouraging businesses to adopt sustainable and socially responsible practices, most notably through its ten principles. UN Environment regularly invites private sector actors to attend meetings and discussions as an observer at its headquarters. The tripartite model gives governments, employers and workers 'equal status' in negotiations. The private sector has also long been a partner in more "invisible" technical bodies that regulate things such as information, aviation, and shipping. Despite existing mechanisms and entry points for increased engagement, private sector actors are asking for greater inclusion at all stages of decision-making on implementation of the 2030 Agenda. The SDG Fund's Private Sector Advisory Group found that businesses want and need to be brought to the table from the very beginning; they should be involved in the development and design of programs on the ground. This new type of partnership entails aligning objectives and expectations from the early stages of programming. A lot of companies want to work with the UN for the SDG not meeting the demand for engagement at the national and local levels. As mentioned by the chief of the UN Conference on Trade and Development (UNCTAD) New York, "There's no hotline to call or publicly available list of focal points within relevant agencies, funds and programs to initiate meaningful discussions."

This problem is exacerbated in countries with smaller UN missions and without the funding to introduce their SMEs to relevant UN actors. To achieve the global partnership envisioned in the 2030 Agenda, the UN needs to engage more with SMEs. While these enterprises provide the majority of employment worldwide, they are traditionally excluded from global supply chains, many of the standard requirements for the private sector to engage with the UN (e.g., reporting mechanisms, compliance with the UN Guiding Principles on Business and Human Rights, conflict assessments, and due-diligence processes) surpass the capabilities and resources of SMEs, further marginalizing them. To address this challenge, the Business and Sustainable Development Commission recommends that governments and large public companies develop sustainability metrics and communication strategies for their procurement processes and requirements that are tailored to SMEs. Answering SMEs' demand for effective, timely engagement should also be a priority for UN country teams. While the UN Global Compact's local networks provide one method of deepening engagement, Officers from the organization admit that only around 30 percent of these networks are at full capacity and that local networks are not fully connected with UN country offices. UN resident coordinators can use their offices to advocate for a closer relationship between governments and local businesses, particularly in countries where there is a lack of trust between the two sectors. In addition, the UN Global Compact's Business for Peace platform which assists companies in implementing responsible business practices in conflict-affected countries, has been working on implementing differentiated reporting mechanisms for SMEs in conflict-affected countries in order to lessen the burden of their engagement. On a broader scale, UN country teams could engage in broader consultations with local private sector representatives in the implementation of the UN Development Assistance Framework to secure the private sector's partnership in achieving national priorities. They could also create platforms for gathering local companies and government representatives to work on joint programs related to the 2030 Agenda.

Transforming the Private Sector into a Partner

The SDGs cannot become a way for companies to repackage. We need to go from embedded corporate social responsibility to seeing companies as key actors for sustainable development.

In order to achieve transformative impact, companies need to embed the principles of the SDGs directly into their business strategies, their long-term objectives, research and development, hiring processes and incentive programs, and all stages of the supply chain. According to the SDG Fund, "In every industry sector, it is these core business investments and activities that offer the greatest potential for achieving sustained results at scale." Sustainable growth will only take place if companies take into account the impact of their activities on society, the environment, governance, and inclusivity when developing their strategies. Consumers are increasingly holding companies accountable and being more conscious of where they put their money. According to a representative from Aviva, "The general public values sustainability more and more consumers trust companies more and employees feel pride when their company acts sustainably in a way that development system in various ways, including benefits society." Because of this increased public through philanthropy and corporate social responsibility (CSR), these approaches have had positive attention, "the private sector used to think that my business is just my business, but now that its results but have not matched the scale, ambition, or changing." By "meeting society's demand for sustainability needed "to transform our world," as called for in the 2030 Agenda. Philanthropy and CSR often remain detached from companies' core solutions to social problems; sustainability brings to companies a competitive advantage that ensures their long-term viability." Business strategies are often designed to offset negative impacts of business operations. CSR often entails a compartmentalized approach to sustainable development that is primarily focused on reducing environmental impact. Moreover, CSR reporting and accountability mechanisms often lack external review and standardized metrics.

This has led to calls for the private sector to transform its approach to sustainable development:

One example is GSMA, the largest association of mobile phone operators. GSMA trains its employees to mentor member companies on the SDGs and communicate that anyone can have an impact and become an agent for sustainable development. Examples of multinational companies starting to embed the SDGs in their business strategies include Siemens's commitment to becoming carbon neutral, Coca-Cola and Nestle's shift toward sustainable, local sourcing of ingredients, and Aviva's efforts to champion sustainable finance in its investments and throughout the financial sector. These decisions are also motivated by the profit companies expect from investing in sustainable practices. The SDGs represent an economic opportunity for businesses, and more of them are arguing in favor of the SDGs not only because they are better for the world but also because they increase returns. It is estimated that achieving the SDGs could open up $12 trillion of market opportunities in just four economic systems food and agriculture, cities, energy and materials, and health and well-being and create 380 million new jobs by 2030. The SDGs make business sense.

In line with these assessments, the CEO of Siemens conveyed that he expects the company's transition to being carbon neutral to be profitable. Coca-Cola's chairman highlighted that when he explained to the board that they could replenish the amount of water they use globally, they accepted it only when he "showed them the algebra" and demonstrated that it helped both their bottom line and the planet. The CEO of Unilever has strongly advocated moving toward sustainable business models, noting that Unilever's brands that have embedded sustainability are growing 30 percent faster than the rest of the company: "This is proving that there is no trade-off between sustainability and profitable growth," he argues. Many companies also see an opportunity to leverage the SDGs to build new markets: "As economic growth in the advanced countries has slowed, multinational corporations are looking to developing countries for the bulk of their growth. That has shifted the priority of development from an afterthought to a central priority of major business leaders.

The SDGs create a common framework for companies looking to identify new suppliers or markets.

Regardless of these positive steps, not all companies are engaging with the 2030 Agenda. According to Ethical Corporation's 2016 'State of Responsible Business Report', more than half of global companies do not plan to engage with the SDGs; though another survey in 2015 it was found that 70 percent plan to embed them into their work within five years. This is a missed opportunity.

Companies that do engage with the SDGs still most often frame their goals within their CSR policies. They relegate the SDGs to silos, tasking them to their sustainability departments rather than incorporating them into core business strategies. According to one CEO, "There is still too much reluctance by business leaders and investors to fully embrace the change to this new type of business model. The focus still tends to be on CSR rather than embedding sustainability at the core of their business. They need to realize that this approach needs to be more than a simple CSR exercise."

Novozymes, a global biotechnology company, provides one example of how to move in this direction. It has embedded its long-term sustainable development targets and incentives into its company purpose and strategy, integrating SDG-linked initiatives throughout the company. To enable greater understanding of and connections between its innovations and their potential impact on the SDGs, Novozymes has developed an SDG impact assessment tool. They are now in the process of forming partnerships with commercial and non-commercial partners to accelerate those innovations: "This comprehensive approach means that everyone at Novozymes has a stake in the SDGs, creating new points of engagement," according to a representative of the company.

Being a partner in implementing the 2030 Agenda also comes with added responsibility for the private sector. For example, SDG target 12.6 "encourages companies, especially large and transnational companies, to adopt sustainable practices and to integrate sustainability information into their reporting cycle." This presents an opportunity for the private sector to showcase what it is doing to turn its visions into reality. But little has been done in this direction so far. There is still a pressing need to strengthen reporting and monitoring. There are no follow-up or review mechanisms in place to monitor the engagement of large companies in achieving the 2030 Agenda, let alone of SMEs. This makes it difficult to measure the existing and expanding contributions of the private sector. One obstacle is the perceived disconnect between businesses and the SDG indicators and targets, which often do not apply to them and are not geared toward a business audience. Translating these into "key performance indicators" that resonate with bottom-line-oriented businesses could help more companies see the merits of the 2030 Agenda and their unique role in achieving it. These different reporting parameters would need to be coherent and to ensure that their language is 'Sustainable Finance: A step toward more responsible investment'.

The financial sector has enormous potential to advance the SDGs: "The biggest impact one can have on the SDGs is how one invest his money," noted a representative of UNCTAD.

One of the fast-track strategies to unlock this potential is the expansion of sustainable finance. Sustainable finance involves integrating environmental, social, and governance criteria into the decisions of financial services companies to account for their impact not only on their clients but also on society as a whole. This is not just an altruistic idea to benefit society; it represents a shift in investors' understanding of their role in society and an investment in their own long-term survival.

The tipping point for industry-wide change toward sustainable finance seems to lie, again, in partnerships. Companies cannot complete this shift alone, especially those operating in multiple markets. The UN can provide a common framework and direction. The approval of a UN resolution on sustainable finance, for example, could "crystallize work in this critical area, especially in improving financial literacy," sending a strong signal to investors that governments are behind this shift.

Another example of a partnership around sustainable finance is the Sustainable Stock Exchanges Initiative co-organized by UNCTAD, the UN Global Compact, the UN Environment Finance Initiative, and the Principles for Responsible Investment. This initiative is a peer-to-peer learning platform for exploring how exchanges, investors, regulators, and companies can enhance corporate transparency and performance on environmental, social, and corporate governance issues and encourage sustainable investment. The initiative has succeeded in getting major stock exchanges worldwide to make a public commitment to sustainability in their markets.

As with corporations more generally, the public is increasingly pressurizing financial services companies to incorporate sustainability into their business strategies. According to a representative of an insurance company, "The largest transfer of wealth is happening now from the baby boomers to the millennial, and the millennial are asking about the impact of their investments." Companies and governments could help by including SDG-related options in employees' retirement plans or pensions, which amounted to $26 trillion in 2015 for countries in the Organization for Economic Co-operation and Development (OECD) investments.

Some positive actions by the UN and its member states to involve the private sector in follow-up and monitoring its contributions must be recognized. Companies have been increasingly invited to participate in the High-Level Political Forum, the body responsible for following up on the 2030 Agenda. Moreover, the UN Global Compact is starting to discuss strengthening its accountability mechanisms through "third-party verification" systems that would guarantee transparency and compliance with the Global Compact principles.

Many national governments are also recognizing the opportunity at hand. Worldwide, member states are involving the private sector in the preparation of their national voluntary reviews. There is also a growth in funding pools that embed the SDGs directly into the application process. In the Netherlands and Denmark, for example, all projects qualifying for government funding at a minimum need to incorporate metrics to evaluate

SDG 8 (decent work and economic growth) and processes to meet SDG 17 (partnerships for the goals).

The Role of the Private Sector in Sustaining Peace

According to the director of the SDG Fund, "Businesses are increasingly seeing the importance of peace and strong institutions as key elements for their success and for the success of communities and stakeholders." But business operations are still not usually associated with peace, even following the launch of the SDGs. A common sentiment amongst people was that peace is beyond the scope of the private sector. Businesses generally understand their role in development more clearly than their role in building inclusive and peaceful societies. While research suggests that a stronger private sector is associated with more peaceful countries, many businesses do not see themselves as active players in building and sustaining peace.

The SDGs can help change that. By providing a common language and shared expectations, goals, and targets, the 2030 Agenda provides an entry point for the private sector to make a positive contribution to peace in a multi-sectoral and multi-dimensional manner. For businesses to thrive, they need to operate in a peaceful environment. When businesses' corporate practices exacerbate conflict, they harm their own interests. In contrast, when they use a "sustaining peace" approach that builds trust among communities and includes local people, they contribute to a more stable environment that enables business and advances their interests.

Going Beyond "Do No Harm"

Multiple, complex dynamics can make it harder to do business in countries under stress, particularly in those simultaneously facing challenges like high unemployment, structural inequality, marginalization of certain segments of society, ethnic or sectarian tensions, and power struggles. There is no 'one-size-fits-all' approach to how the private sector can navigate these challenges. Nonetheless, one thing is certain. Solely injecting money into such countries will not help build peace; in fact, it can be harmful. Therefore, it is crucial that all business operations and investments are context-specific and that they "do no harm." While many companies have embraced the need to reduce the negative environmental impact of their operations, less progress has been made on reducing negative social impact. For example, corporate practices may inadvertently fuel tensions by indirectly legitimizing armed groups that control certain territories. Similarly, an infusion of jobs and contracts, if it benefits one social group over another, can intensify existing or latent conflicts or perpetuate structural inequalities. It is therefore critical to undertake a conflict assessment when planning such operations to avoid contributing to existing conflict dynamics. But solely adopting a "do no harm" approach is not enough. The focus should not be only on how to avoid fueling conflict but also on how to support the factors underpinning peace, in line with the sustaining peace resolutions. This requires mapping the key actors that work for peace and benefit from conflict and identifying the factors contributing to a society's resilience that could be strengthened and marshaled to make the private sector more inclusive.

Such an approach should be deliberate. It requires businesses to be intentional in their contributions to prevention and peace building rather than simply making sure they "do no harm." Moreover, a sustaining peace approach should be transformative rather than transactional. It should seek to promote inclusive national ownership by empowering national governments and involving all sectors of society, including local companies and communities. Movement toward a sustaining peace approach could build on previous efforts such as the UN Guiding Principles on Business and Human Rights, developed in 2011. These principles not only aim to help companies identify how to reduce the risk of human rights abuses along their entire supply chains but also create a "formal responsibility" for the private sector to uphold human rights while conducting business.

Strengthening Public Institutions

A central aspect of a "sustaining peace" approach that promotes inclusive national ownership lies in establishing a trustworthy, synergetic, and mutually beneficial relationship with national initiatives to achieve the SDGs. Government leadership and strengthened institutions will be key to providing the adequate framework for businesses to jointly work on the 2030 Agenda.

The private sector can never replace the primacy of governments as the central policymakers behind the 2030 Agenda. Responsibility for following up on the targets and indicators of the 2030 Agenda rests in the hands of governments, from national to local authorities. As such, businesses, whether foreign or local, need to develop strong relationships with governments at the national and local levels.

But this is often challenging. In countries under stress, state institutions and legal frameworks are often weak and lack transparency and accountability. For domestic and international companies, navigating these fragile governance systems is a major difficulty. As one UN official highlighted, "How can a company manage to comply with the rule of law when the rule of law does not exist in the country". How can a company promote governance where the state is fragile and governance is divided between the official government and different armed groups".

At the same time, businesses can take advantage of lax governmental institutions, further contributing to instability and economic stagnation. For instance, they can diminish the role of the public sector by pushing for policies such as deregulation and privatization. Corporations can also undermine national governments by evading or avoiding taxes. As noted by the Civil Society Reflection Group on the 2030 Agenda, for example, "The failure of corporations to pay taxes in the countries where they operate is a major reason for governments' lack of fiscal space to implement policies that would protect and promote women's human rights."

Although the private sector's contribution is indispensable, governments need to be in the driving seat of the 2030 Agenda. Similarly, there must be limitations on what responsibilities the private sector can take on. According to a senior vice president of the World Bank, "At the end of the day, the private sector is the private sector and the government is the government". The comparative advantage of government is to apply rules, put in standards, and follow the execution of measures; the comparative advantage of the private sector is efficiency and competition." The key is to establish clear limits and promote inclusive partnerships that are mutually beneficial and leverage each sector's core competencies. Multilateral institutions can help facilitate such partnerships by advocating and working with governments to establish a good business environment for competition, consumer protections, and adequate regulatory frameworks. But the challenge is not only having adequate regulations, it is also having the capacity to implement and enforce them.

One area where businesses are actively partnering with governments and civil society is in the fight against corruption. For example, in 2009, following a bribery scandal, Siemens established a "vigorous integrity system in the company" to address and prevent corruption, which it is sharing with other businesses. In partnership with the World Bank, the company has set up a $100 million fund to support anti-corruption initiatives by non-governmental organizations in countries where corruption is a major hindrance to sustainable development.

Making the Private Sector More Inclusive at the Local Level

As part of implementing the 2030 Agenda, companies need to ensure that their operations are inclusive. Businesses have a greater potential to contribute to peace if they adopt hiring practices that foster inclusive economic growth, ensure equal pay for women, and shift toward sustainable production. This is particularly important for small and medium enterprises (SMEs), which contribute up to 60 percent of total employment and up to 40 percent of national income in emerging economies. They also have closer ties with communities. The interest of SMEs in building peace is direct: if their own communities are fraught with violence and crime, they lack the conditions needed to build a successful business. These enterprises have more knowledge of the local context and can adopt hiring practices that reflect their community's needs and characteristics. Toward this end, larger companies could promote the development of SMEs at the local level by partnering and sharing information with them and making SMEs their preferred providers for outsourcing and backbone services.

To move toward inclusivity, companies no matter their size need to make sure they have inclusive policies toward youth and women. Growth that excludes these groups could have adverse effects on peace.

If youth are unemployed and disengaged, they can become more vulnerable to recruitment into organized crime or violent extremist groups. On the contrary, meaningful engagement via employment, entrepreneurship opportunities, and access to the decision-making sphere can help make youth agents for sustainable development and peace. Research by the Institute for Economics and Peace on the connection between youth development, social entrepreneurship, and sustaining peace found that there is a strong correlation between positive peace and the Youth Development Index. Historically, businesses have often hired women as inexpensive labor, which can undermine gender equality. As noted by the Civil Society Reflection Group on the 2030 Agenda, "Women's lower wages and poorer labor conditions have worked as an major advantage for corporations." promoting gender equality and women's empowerment instead of exploiting cheap female labor, companies could promote stability. Gender equality is a strong predictor of a state's peacefulness. Businesses can put this approach into practice in a number of ways, including by improving the gender balance in their labor force, providing equal pay to women and men, ensuring work place safety, and opening spaces for women in leadership positions.

Promoting employment for women in Bangladesh

Many households headed by widowed, divorced, or abandoned women in Bangladesh are afflicted by extreme poverty. These women are often unemployed or employed in low-skill, low-wage jobs, causing them to be stuck in poverty traps. The SDG Fund therefore launched a joint program to promote employment and the future employability of poor rural women in Bangladesh. This program brings together efforts by local businesses, local governments, and UN agencies in the country. It offers a scalable model for lifting women out of poverty. The initiative starts by providing public work opportunities and cash transfers for the beneficiaries. This safety net is accompanied by a training program supported by the International Labor Organization on vocational skills, local leadership, and saving mechanisms that help them transition to market-based employment. The private sector is directly involved by engaging local SMEs to provide skills training based on their demand and job placement.

This program underscores the positive connections between women's inclusion, poverty reduction, and peaceful societies. It also highlights the power of SMEs to promote inclusive growth. By facilitating public-private partnerships with these enterprises (SDG 17), it is generating job opportunities that empower women, build the resilience of households, and increase economic inclusion (SDGs 5 and 8), which ultimately makes the community more inclusive and peaceful (SDG 16).

Building Trust with Communities

The history of relations between businesses and the communities where they operate is complicated. Large-scale projects, particularly in the extractive industries, often have had negative impacts, leading to widespread displacement, conflict, and violations of the rights of indigenous populations.

Companies can have a positive impact by providing jobs, heightening demand for locally produced goods and services, investing in infrastructure and social services, and increasing government resources through taxes and royalties. For example, UNCTAD suggests that if companies build roads, water systems, energy facilities, or other infrastructure to support production, they should give preferential access to local communities. But often companies cannot meet high expectations such as providing full employment and investing all the returns locally. The 2030 Agenda provides a framework to better meet these expectations.

Companies need to establish trust from the start by having open and transparent communication channels to set clear expectations and provide spaces for community members to express their grievances and priorities. Building relationships with community leaders is also an important entry point to understanding the local context, ensuring peaceful interactions, and ultimately building trust a prerequisite for any effective partnership.

Unlocking the Trillions Needed to Achieve the SDGs

In order to bridge the gap between the private sector and efforts to build and sustain peace, there is a need to incentivize private investment in countries where capital is most needed.

It is estimated that the amount needed to achieve the SDGs by 2030 is $3.9 trillion a year, meaning that continued investment at 2014 levels would leave a $2.5 trillion gap. Private investment is essential to closing that gap. But in many countries under stress, lack of business competitiveness, transparency, economic productivity, and strong regulatory systems thwart investment, leading to stagnant economic growth and increased unemployment and limiting prospects for stability. On the one side we need to have a stable environment, otherwise one does not get the investment, but at the same time one needs the investment to get a stable environment."

How can businesses be incentivized to invest in places where the rule of law is lax, security conditions are volatile or dangerous, and financial risks are high. Risks must be mitigated, projects must be made bankable, and achieving the SDGs must be made appealing to the private sector in order to access and leverage the trillions needed to achieve the 2030 Agenda.

Many companies struggle to identify entry points. Particularly in countries under stress, the cost of carrying out a thorough risk assessment can outweigh the level of return, making it difficult for bottom-line-oriented companies to justify such investments to their shareholders. The real challenge is thus scaling up projects. Companies do not want to invest their money in small project. The problem is not the lack of money; it is the lack of scale. Innovative methods to scale up projects are needed.

But many countries under stress lack the capacity and mechanisms to scale up and attract large investments. According to a representative of UN Environment, "We need to talk about the absolute imperative of building capacity to formulate sustainable, bankable projects. We need to help countries to understand how important that is and help them to find the necessary expertise and support." One way governments can do this is by increasing public investment, as "investors are likely to invest in countries that have the highest existing public investment."

While governments can create a more enabling environment for public investment, international institutions can also encourage private investment, helping to bridge the gap between small-scale investments on the ground and the large-scale investments needed. For example, international financial institutions, regional banks, or donors can provide collateral investment to reduce the risks faced by private investors.

Blended Finance

Companies often do not find the levels of return needed to invest in countries under stress due to the risk involved and the challenge blended finance can help overcome. The OECD defines blended finance as the strategic use of public funds to mobilize private sector investment for emerging and Least Developed Countries (LDCs). By using strategic public or philanthropic policies recommended that development partners "set up and strengthen initiatives to support investment in least developed countries such as investment in least developed countries like insurance, philanthropic funding to catalyze private sector investments, blended finance "can target a risk that the private sector is unwilling or unable to take guarantees and preferential financing programmes and private enterprise funds." The focus should not be on one-off programs. In order to be scaled up through private investment, projects require long-term, self-sustaining funding models and an increase in the diversity of investors.

The research study offers practical tools to promote the involvement of local and international companies in countries under stress in order to achieve the 2030 Agenda. These tools can help to reduce risk the number-one reason companies avoid investing in countries under stress. These tools have something in common; all the financial instruments are based on collaboration between national and international actors. Although blended finance is not new, it has been gaining increasing traction as an important tool to mobilize new capital to achieve the SDGs. In fact, the 2030 Agenda recognizes that "an important use of international public finance, including Official Development Assistance (ODA), is to catalyze additional resource mobilization from other sources, public and private."

It is estimated that leveraging public and philanthropic funding could lead to as much as a tenfold increase in overall investment. Based on conservative estimates, there is already at least $25.4 billion invested in over seventy-four blended finance funds and facilities, in addition to hundreds of individual projects receiving blended finance in emerging and frontier markets. Many of these are projects in infrastructure, climate change solutions and agriculture sectors that are critical for development and that suffer from the largest shortfall in funding. Because blended finance operates at the intersection between fully commercial and subsidized or grant-dependent projects, it can make them more self-reliant, viable, and scalable.

Matching Funds in the SDG Fund

The SDG Fund uses blended finance through a matching funds system, which requires that every financial contribution made by the SDG Fund is matched at least one-to-one by the joint program partners. The SDG Fund relies on matching funds provided by national and local governments, international donors, and the private sector. By involving national partners who often have a greater stake in the success and sustainability of programs this model builds trust and fosters national ownership. The private sector co-invests and co-designs with the government and UN agencies from the beginning. Furthermore, 56 percent of the SDG Fund's overall program budget comes from matching funds. Thus, every dollar invested in the SDG Fund has generated $2.36 in the program budget. So far, 3.5 million people have benefited from the SDG Fund's twenty-two joint programs, including 1.4 million directly and 2.2 million indirectly. But to effectively tap into the potential of blended finance, more data needs to be made available. For example, convergence has been working to provide information and connect investors to execute blended finance transactions. But there is still not enough information on risk and return.

Blended finance can also unlock domestic private investments. As noted by an official at UN Environment, "The risk perception of the domestic investor is considerably more nuanced than that of the foreign private investor, and the amount of de-risking through public resources that would be needed is considerably less." Even smaller-scale blended finance mechanisms that may not attract large international investors could therefore still mobilize domestic investors.

However, there is a risk that blended finance subsidizes investments that businesses would have made on their own, without any need for public funding. To prevent this, governments and philanthropic organizations need to make sure the project would not have happened without the added support that blended finance provides.

The World Bank Group, one of the largest channels of blended finance from multilateral and bilateral donors, uses the cascade approach through its private sector Window to prevent this from occurring. This approach involves first considering private sector solutions, then blended finance, and only then public sector solutions. As described by the senior vice president of the World Bank, "the cascade approach to investment decision-making encourages private sector participation, while leveraging and preserving scarce public dollars for critical public investments. If commercial financing is available, that is the preferred course. If it is absent, market failures should be next addressed. If those efforts are unsuccessful, risk instruments should be utilized along with matching capital to try to encourage private investment. Finally, if absolutely necessary, then public and concessional financing should be used.

The aim of this approach is to deploy public resources strategically to expand the pool of projects that can be financed with commercial and private capital.

However, when the cascade approach is used with the aim of empowering the public sector and benefiting communities, it can be a useful tool. The cascade approach highlights the need to differentiate roles and capacities between governments and businesses and to use the comparative advantage of each sector to accelerate sustainable development and avoid crowding out investment that would occur without state intervention.

Pooling Mechanisms

Pooling mechanisms are another strategy for scaling up projects. By pooling the underlying assets of a portfolio of projects or grouping related projects together, the overall returns are higher, making the investment more attractive. Similarly, involving diverse groups of investors with different appetites for risks in a syndicate arrangement can lower the risk to a more manageable level. Under pooling mechanisms, financial entities like private equity funds can gather several projects and offer them as an aggregated product to more risk-averse investors like pension funds or insurance companies. Instead of making investors decide whether to invest in each of many individual projects, they can invest a larger amount in many projects at the same time. Even if one fails, the investors will not lose all their money. Furthermore, pooling eliminates the need to conduct due diligence for each project individually, thus lowering the costs of the overall investment and enhancing the net return.

Pooled financing mechanisms are rightly being explored at the municipal level in developing countries such as Colombia and South Africa as well as by many OECD countries to fund investments in water and sanitation, energy, transport, and telecommunications infrastructure. Sub-national pooled financing mechanisms provide joint access to private capital markets at advantageous terms for borrowers (in this case, local governments) that share similar missions and credit characteristics but lack the financial scope and scale, expertise, and credit history to access credit markets independently.

Micro Finance

Microfinance can be thought of as the very first rung on the ladder of scaling up projects; if people do not have the capacity to borrow, many of the SDGs would be set to fail. The 2030 Agenda recognizes the importance of financial inclusion, including through access to microfinance (SDG 1 on poverty reduction). More than 2 billion people lack access to basic financial services such as savings accounts, loans, or insurance. Because the cost of setting up microfinance facilities on the ground is high, digital finance has become an important source of microfinance in many developing countries.

Pooling and blending to unlock private finance for the climate, biodiversity, and jobs in Indonesia

An example of using multiple tools to overcome the barriers to private investment is the 'Tropical Landscapes Financing Facility' in Indonesia. This is a partnership between a major international bank, an international asset management company, farmers' collectives, a major bilateral aid agency, the government of Indonesia, and UN Environment, all playing well-defined and complementary roles.

According to a representative of UN Environment, "This program translates massive international private capital flows into financing for small-scale bankable projects on the ground. It enables the transition to scale." The program will pool small individual projects to bring them to a financeable scale. It will also use blended finance instruments such as loan and grant funds to unlock private finance. In addition, the program will provide access to long-term finance at affordable rates, which is essential for small producers. Investments will focus on renewable energy production and sustainable landscape management to reduce deforestation and forest degradation and restore degraded land.

The aim is to promote economic development while helping Indonesia meets its targets under the 'Paris Agreement on climate change'. The program aims to trigger progress across a number of targets of the 2030 Agenda, including addressing climate change, protecting biodiversity, fostering renewable energy, and promoting economic growth. Access to financial services is key to helping the most vulnerable people build assets and protect against shocks. Microfinance can boost entrepreneurship and accelerate job creation. However, the microfinance industry can have difficulty absorbing the vast volumes of private sector capital that global organizations can mobilize. As highlighted by the head of a private sector micro finance initiative, microfinance is an effort that "puts women in the center" and, in doing so, contributes to gender equality (SDG 5). There are 1.1 billion women who lack access to bank accounts, making women the largest group of financially excluded people.

Although the link between financial inclusion and development has been widely established, microfinance cannot only be about borrowing. According to one company's CSR representative, "Now the challenge is not about getting the loans, but how to manage money. It's about building people's capacity because they need to be able to pay the loan." Although microfinance can help scale up investments, particularly by strengthening SMEs, not everyone who gets a loan will necessarily become a job generator. Microfinance needs to come hand in hand with practical financial education to address criticisms that many borrowers end up not being able to pay back loans.

Development Impact Bonds

Another emerging model for incentivizing investment in countries under stress is development impact bonds. This type of results-based financing has a high potential to mitigate risk for the private sector. Under this model, an outcome funder third party such as a donor agency or foundation repays private investors with a return, contingent upon the achievement of agreed upon outcomes.

Policy Conclusions and Recommendations

The 2030 Agenda provides an unprecedented opportunity for collaborating to address the most pressing global challenges. For this collaboration to be effective, the current framework for cooperation between the UN, its member states, civil society, and the private sector needs to change. This requires clarifying the connections between businesses, sustainable development, and peace; understanding that businesses and the public sector have different objectives and leveraging these differences to maximize the comparative advantage of each; engaging businesses and civil society more directly in co-designing, co-investing in, and co-implementing policies and programs related to the 2030 Agenda; and systematically monitoring and reporting on the cumulative contributions of businesses to achieving the targets and indicators of the 2030 Agenda. The following are specific recommendations to make this partnership a reality which is reflected in Chapter II.

CHAPTER II

BUSINESSES AND ROLE OF LARGE COMPANIES IN ACHIEVING UNITED NATIONS SUSTAINABLE DEVELOPMENT GOALS

Businesses should embed the SDGs in their core business strategies

This involves integrating the SDGs in supply chains, practices, and policies. In practice, such a strategy could involve sourcing products locally and sustainably, moving toward zero waste, employing more women and youth, providing equal pay to women and men, ensuring adequate workplace safety, and opening spaces for women, particularly those from underrepresented groups in leadership positions. Businesses should also create options for SDG-aligned investment portfolios for employee retirement accounts and pensions.

Businesses should improve reporting on their contributions to the SDGs

Businesses should work with the UN to fine-tune a common language that connects the SDG targets with business performance indicators. In addition, businesses should report on long-term SDG- related metrics along with them bottom-line profits.

Businesses should expand engagement with UN headquarters

The private sector should use the High-Level Political Forum on Sustainable Development and UN General Assembly summits on the follow-up and review of the 2030 Agenda as opportunities to further expand engagement with the UN and its member states and participation in decision-making fora. The UN and member states should reciprocate by inviting more companies to these fora.

Global leaders should emphasize that the SDGs are good for business

Investing in a more peaceful and sustainable society is also an investment in sustainability for businesses. Global leaders should better communicate to businesses that the SDGs represent an economic opportunity and can help them grow their bottom lines.

The UN, governments, and large companies should increase engagement with small and medium enterprises

Small and medium enterprises (SMEs) should play a bigger role in efforts to achieve the SDGs. UN country teams should create new mechanisms to engage with SMEs that take into account their more limited human capital. National governments should invite SMEs to participate in the preparation and implementation of the national voluntary review processes. Large companies should also involve SMEs in their investments at the local level by partnering and sharing information with them and making SMEs their preferred providers for outsourcing and backbone services.

Governments and businesses should work together closely in implementing the SDGs

Businesses should support national governments in strengthening public institutions, including by developing and implementing regulations and practices that promote sustainable development. UN resident coordinators should also advocate for a closer relationship between governments and businesses, and UN country teams should act as platforms for gathering companies and government representatives to work on joint programmes related to the 2030 Agenda. The private sector can be a partner not only in pursuing sustainable development but also in sustaining peace. Expanding operations and investing in countries under stress can benefit the private sector by unlocking new opportunities for profit while also benefiting countries that lack capital and resources. An inclusive private sector can help boost economic growth, provide employment opportunities, and increase stability. However, injecting resources without assessing the impact they can have on conflict and peace can be more harmful than beneficial. The following recommendations aim to strengthen the link between the private sector and peace:

Businesses should take a sustaining peace approach to their operations

Businesses need to comply with the "does no harm" principle throughout all their operations, but that is not enough; they should also adopt a "sustaining peace" approach. This entails assessing not only how their work can avoid contributing to conflict but also how it can support efforts to build and sustain peace. Operations and investments should be context-specific, people-centered, and deliberately crafted to be transformative rather than transactional and to strengthen public institutions and local communities.

Businesses should build trust with communities

From the start, businesses should have open and transparent communication channels with the communities where they work, setting up clear expectations and providing space for community members to express their grievances and priorities. Businesses should partner with community leaders and use existing community structures as the main entry points for engagement. This would allow them to build trust, better understand the local context, and foster peaceful interactions.

Businesses should strive to be more inclusive

An inclusive private sector has greater potential to contribute to peace. Businesses should adopt more inclusive hiring practices. They should also foster more inclusive economic growth by targeting youth and women as the main beneficiaries of their operations. This is particularly important for SMEs, which are the largest job generators and have closer ties with communities.

Funding the 2030 Agenda is not the problem; the resources exist but are not accessible through traditional investment models. The risk associated with investing in countries under stress and lack of scalability has impeded private investment. The following recommendations aim to address these impediments to investment in countries under stress:

The UN, governments, and businesses should **partner to scale up investments in countries under stress.** To attract resources from the private sector and unlock the trillions needed to achieve the SDGs, the private sector, the UN, its member states, and other relevant actors should further explore innovative financial mechanisms. These mechanisms include blended finance, pooling mechanisms, and development impact bonds.

The new partnership between governments, the UN, and businesses should not focus on one-off programs

Projects require long-term, self-sustaining funding models and a wider diversity of investors.

CHAPTER III

ROLE OF INTERNATIONAL ORGANIZATIONS IN GLOBAL ECONOMIC GOVERNANCE

The challenge of international organizations and their role in the global economy remains in the midst of global economic governance approach, although it seemed utopian at first and regarded as too ambitious in redefining the international system. This research study aims to underline and reassess the role of international organizations in the new paradigm of global economic governance. The approach is a more theoretical one, with emphasis on results and future research. The key results are related to some aspects of redefining the global economic governance in terms of international organizations. The main added value is the pragmatic approach of the role of international organizations and its formal relationship with the global economic governance. Over the last two decades, the international community has increasingly become so interconnected and interdependent due to the rapid progress in technology and the development of economic integration processes.

The recent economic crisis has revealed the weaknesses and shortages of cooperation in the global economy and only the diplomatic consensus has led to the adoption of urgent solutions. But as the global economy seems to be out of recession, at least in certain parts of the world, states have begun to focus on fiscal and social policies in order to overcome the continuing effects of the crisis, and the desire to improve cooperation relationships and global economic governance seems to be in decline.

The international community has paid a very high price for satisfying itself with the financial and macroeconomic risks as advertised, but the economic risks seem to multiply every day waiting for proactive answers. But how can global governance be redesigned in terms of architecture without taking into account the critical role of international organizations? When states were dominant actors on the international stage and major policy decisions were taken by only a few of them, the progresses in international cooperation tended to be quantified through creating new institutions and intergovernmental organizations.

But the current problems show that efforts to strengthen international cooperation should focus on creating new institutions and international rules, to modernizing the existing framework for a greater integration of governmental framework in policy decisions.

The research study tries to highlight the main elements that define the current role of international organizations in global economic governance, the change of paradigm and the concept of legitimacy in international relations. The study presents some elements of defining the international organizations, a brief history of the modern economic system, the paradigmatic role of international organizations in the current global economic governance and addressing the concept of legitimacy in the actual configuration of international relations. The study also attempts to highlight some elements that draw new paradigm of global economic governance, with subjects as multilateral agreements, voting system or leadership, as well as some international proposals to emphasize the awareness of economic system to current challenges and opportunities.

International Organizations: A General View

International organizations are important actors in the critical episodes of international politics, with power in mediation, dispute resolution, peace keeping, applying sanctions and others. They also help in managing various key areas of international concern, from global health policy to the monetary policies around the world (Abbott and Snidal, 1998).

An international organization can be defined as 'an institutional agreement between members of an international system in order to achieve objectives according to systemic conditions, reflecting attributes, aspirations and concerns of its members' (Hanrieder, 1966). And what gives the basic rule of them is the sovereignty of the nation-state (Barkin and Cronin, 2009).

In terms of the concept of global governance promoted by the international organizations, this was originally based on raw power, but has evolved to legitimacy and customs (Keohane and Nye, 2001).

Brief History of the System

Modern international system has three main architectural features, built in overlapping phases over time. The first stage concerns the definition of the state as a primary tool of decision in international relations. The Treaty of Westphalia in 1648 established peace in Europe after decades of conflicts and bloody wars. Then it was set up the basis of global dialogue based on national sovereignty, each territory seeking political solutions to their religious problems. But the nation-state was consolidated as an expression of sovereignty in the 19th century and defined as an important factor in global policy-making process that took place in the 20th century.

The second stage refers to the agreements between states. This development is associated with the Congress of Vienna in 1815, where European powers negotiated the end of two decades of war and redrawn the political map of the continent. The agreements signed during Cold War and even today, are considered to be projections of diplomatic consensus that stabilized Europe in the 19th century.

The third stage consists of the architecture of multilateral system, having in its core the United Nations. Built largely in the period after the Second World War, it has antecedents in the post-war period by creating the League of Nations and the International Labor Organization. Conferences at Bretton Woods, Dumbarton Oaks or San Francisco developed plans for building a wide range of universal rules and specialized institutions in order to promote international cooperation in economic, political and security areas.

These three main elements of the system will remain important pillars of international relations for a long period of time. But many scholars consider them to be exceeded in the whole series of economic, political, technological and social changes, which often led to debates on the legitimacy and efficiency in decision making process at international level.

During the last six decades, international organizations have extended and reviewing their mandates and objectives, reaching the global level through the number of members, thus being among the favorite subjects of criticism for accelerating the globalization, failure of their missions or superficial supervision and liberalization of international trade by providing the framework for the negotiations and formalizing trade agreements (Zohal, 2011).

After the Cold War, the institutions of global economic governance have become the favorite subject of criticism. While globalizations and systemic risk awareness led to the need for global governance, the form it took it is no longer adequate to the current challenges, which goes to an increasing sentiment of dissatisfaction about the multilateral order, and then to the crisis of multilateralism. The favorable global institutions do not work either individually or collectively (McGrew, 2011).

Paradigmatic Role of International Organizations

But why states use international organizations as engines for cooperation. Some issues are raised by their structure and operations, and also by international relations theories involving these complex phenomena. The independence of these organizations depends on states, because they can limit or extend their autonomy, interfering in their activity, restructure or dissolve them. They sometimes collide with the sovereignty of the state when they create new structures for regulating cross-border relationships.

One of the main reasons why states want to establish or participate as members of international organizations is related to the fact that they delegate authority in matters that require expertise, knowledge, information, time and resources that are not available at all times (Wouters and de Man, 2009).

International organizations can be a complement to national prevailing paradigm, being an expression of denationalization policies (Zürn, 2004). This is an evident fact by supranational and transnational characteristics of undermining national decisions, using the principle of international cooperation. But the politicization of these decisions brings again into question their need for legitimacy.

Two very important features make the difference between international organizations and other type of organizations: centralizations of power and decision-making autonomy. Both have political effects beyond the simple effectiveness of the already taken decisions, because they resemble so much with governments or private companies. International organizations carry out actions that enjoy a sort of legitimacy and affect the legitimacy of the state activity. Even centralization may alter the perceptions of the states in the context of complex interactions between them (Ostrom, 1990).

The centralization outlines the political context of interactions between states. International organizations provide forums for neutral, depoliticized and specific discussions in a much more effective way than any other agreements. They outline the specific terms of the ongoing interactions between states and try balancing the relationships between stronger and weaker states, between interests and knowledge.

The organizational structure influences the evolution of interstate cooperation and adapts itself to specific circumstances. Most organizations perform functions to support cooperation between conferences dealing with very important issues, as well as implementing a set of regulations (Williamson, 1985). International standards can be addressed as expectations of head of states about international relations.

The Legitimacy of International Organizations

Legitimacy, as concept, was an integral part of political thought for a long time, but only recently has come to the attention of specialists in international relations (Mulligan, 2006). International specialty literature addresses legitimacy as being related to certain criteria that confer continuity and trust. Some well-known researchers say that international organizations seek to establish solid connections between their activities and social values system to which they belong, this links representing their legitimacy (Dowling and Pfeffer, 1975, Buchanan and Keohane, 2006). Others say that legitimacy lies in the means by which to achieve the specific goal (Lawrence, 2008). What is clear is the fact that most researchers have concluded upon the legitimacy problems that international organizations face as threatening the global economic balance, along with other crucial elements (Clark, 2003). When concerns about legitimacy decrease, the system itself is flawed and solutions must be found really quickly.

International organizations participate as independent and neutral actors on the global stage and can transform the relationships between states, increasing the efficiency and legitimacy of their individual or collective decisions. This feature requires the short or long term balanced actions depending on the interest of both sides: powerful states will not join any organization they cannot influence and small countries will not join any organization whose decisions undermine their sovereignty (Bradford and Linn, 2007).

Authoritarian states are reluctant to allow international organizations in taking decisions for them, decisions that interfere with their national policies. States which are undemocratic and unstable and tend to limit the presence of organizations within their territory, states can even be against their participation in global economic governance. Global governance is strengthened only if it fits the internal profile of dominant countries (Cowhey, 1993).

The main attributes of international organizations continue to be in the first line for facilitating negotiations and implementing agreements, dispute resolution, offering technical assistance and developing rules. But the most important thing remains their neutrality, impartiality and independence (Griffin, 2003). Neutrality enables organizations to act as mediators between states and to implement their decisions. Impartiality resides on the fact that neither part is favored whatever the subject is nor independence resides on the fact that international organizations can take decisions for themselves.

It is undeniable that international organizations can take decisions that bind on member states through predictable mechanism and pursuing their interests (Wouters and de Man, 2009).

Decision-making processes vary between consensus, vote and unanimous vote. The most common form of decision-making is consensus, involving further discussions to reach general agreement rather than forcing the decision by voting process. While the member states have certain reservations about the discussions or negotiations, they are forced to make concessions to each other in order to reach an agreement. If consensus cannot be reached, the last resort is unanimous voting or qualified majority voting.

There is a gap between demand, responsibility and jurisdiction of global governance and its institutional capacity to take decisions and implement effective solutions for global problems. This is associated with diminishing expectations that global institutions seem to reach and political demands are addressed, in part because of the lack of resources and because governments cannot deliver properly their institutional capacity (Moravcsik, 2004, Bradford and Linn, 2007).

Most global institutions are unable to take a firm decision and hence the exiting pressing problems, as climate change or financial system reform, that face failure in advancing collective actions. These systemic failures lead to widening the disparities between promised collective actions and what really comes, being clear the limited progress of submission of the Millennium Development Goals.

These deficiencies in the legitimacy and effectiveness exacerbate each other. The countries feel more and more disconnected from international institutions, greater being the tendency to invest in institutions to be successful. The international system needs structural renovation to allow adapting to a global community that is different from the last century existing one.

This problem of legitimacy reveals the question whether legislation as a whole may be able to solve the fundamental dilemma of global capitalism (Tshuma, 2000). The crises of legitimacy can be solved only through reconciliation and communication (Reus-Smith, 2007). Research must continue in defining efficiently the concept of legitimacy and how this can be relevant in terms of its implications (Mulligan, 2006).

Criticizing International Organizations

Most of the current discussions about international organizations refer to the legitimacy and effectiveness of the decisions (Ziegler and Bonzon, 2007). The problem of legitimacy is directly related to the influence of the international organizations and often to state sovereignty. The principle of consensual decision-making is the main subject of critics, with it being argued that they shall be made only at formal level and must reflect the power relations between states, taking the form of a weighted voting under major interests. Informal practices that lead to a decision involve the emergence of some specific groups with some sort of composition, who deliberately exclude other countries (Kim, 2009).

The principle of consensus practiced within the international organization has always meant that all parties have to agree upon a specific issue, but in practice this voting system can be hidden; reality proves that the voting share of wealthier countries is more important than that of poorer countries (Low, 2011).

For historical reasons, many being highly criticized by the developing world, the system is tilted in favor of the rich and powerful countries. For example, whenever developing countries have the chance to gain from free trade, they have confronted quotas or voluntary export restrictions, dumping, safeguards or other forms of limitations. Moreover, instead of focusing on enhancing consumer welfare, the trading system strongly supports manufacturers or exporters, leading to protectionism. Much of the criticism results from the perception that trade was raised to a very high rank, while other values were slaughtered (Guzman, 2004).

Despite differences of perspectives, critics and supporters agree that international cooperation is needed to tackle trade and non-trade issues, such as the environmental problems, intellectual property, investments, health, international finances, modern industrialization, and crises and so on.

The isolationist approach of most of the international organizations ignores the wishes of member countries, concluding with building a different kind of agreements in their detriment, this resulting in rules and norms that rule out concern and wishes to correct the failures of environmental or social issues. One cannot speak about coordination as long as rules always prevail over other agreements and hold the monopoly on international cooperation (Pauwelyn, 2005).

Many countries feel excluded or left behind by the decisions of the international organizations and for the most of the poor countries, participation in the international system remains a distant dream. For example, the international trade system is perceived as a fortress, all the discussions being held behind closed doors and favoring the powerful producers and exporters. The international organizations are seen as closed systems and those who are within those are bounded to their commitments taken in "packages", with no way out or a way to comment upon them, because of the economic reality or simply because of an implementation mechanism more and more strict. And this results in the lack of legitimacy, poor support and a lack of loyalty to the values that underline the system itself (Sutherland and all, 2004).

Most of the critics relate easily to the existing democratic deficit within the international organizations (Elsig, 2007). Unlike the early period of their existence, the lack of legitimacy of these organizations is no longer offset by progress towards globalization. Cooperation in an anarchic era seemed easier than nowadays, in an environment governed by rules and procedures. Increased political participation and the insistence of the members to veto decisions becomes suffocating in further liberalization and increased welfare, but also in preventing the adoption of the reforms needed to balance the system and being in favor of developing countries.

The international organizations have changed the nature, purpose and structure of multilateralism and globalization. They have become the main target of the lobby groups and civil society, fact which led to excessive politicization (Mercurio, 2007). Critics say that the big number of members do not easily allow the organization to reach a consensus or to effectively address the burning issues of the 21st century, this leading to blockages and disagreements during negotiations (Sun, 2011).

The New Paradigm of Global Economic Governance

The recent problems that international system have been faced led to the need in addressing the dilemma related to international agreements and institutions, whether they are viable and meet the needs of the 21st century (Stiglitz, 1999).

Researchers say that they have been facing a real paradox in the approach to this new paradigm of global economic governance: the more seriously we take the concept of global economic governance, the more all its substance runs away and begins to contradict the general knowledge (Smouts, 2002). We live a moment of reaffirmation of a known and long analyzed issue; international organizations face tensions between different point of views about what rules, norms and procedures seem to be fair in the context of global decision-making process (Franceschet, 2002).

Strengthening the international cooperation and governance is not about just institutional arrangements and incentives. The focus is also on values. The international system must be redefined not only in terms of institutional architecture, but also in terms of social architecture, social institutions having the potential to inspire consistent values for an increasingly independent society.

The voting system and the leadership of key institutions must be adapted appropriately with the increase of emerging powers. The world population is getting more informed about international challenges, and it becomes even more aware about the fact that the most important priorities are translated into immediate actions.

In the same time, the proliferation of influential actors has complicated efforts in achieving a multilateral agreement even in areas already discussed about, leading to the conclusion that interdependence has not only led to increasing political challenges, but also in delivering effective international cooperation. In particular, the structural deficiencies of these actors have revealed also limitations in transparency and consistency of decision-making process.

Every architectural innovation starts from some basic principles in order to be ensured as the fundamental interests of maintaining the system. Fortunately, the proposals for reform of global economic governance remain valid and do not require major changes. Global Economic Forum provided public reports that list some proposals on redefining global economic governance to the current challenges of the global economy that are worthy to be taken into account (WEF, 2010): redefining the international system according to the multiple faces of governmental cooperation; strengthening the role of states as basis in decision-making process, while the geometry of cooperation itself takes into account the non-governmental organizations; the implementation of this geometry in a pragmatic way, result oriented, for accelerating the progress of individual and global challenges; specific initiatives to enhance legitimacy, participations and responsibility of the state centered system; extending the international cooperation through value exchange, with profound implications on global objectives.

The renovation of the international system in the ways proposed above would allow the international community to accelerate progress in individual and global challenges. By increasing the interaction between international organizations and civil society (Schwab, 2008), personal and professional responsibility is going to grow in the international system, being one of the key elements of strengthening the international cooperation.

Conclusion

Changes and challenges in the current global economic governance are extremely diverse and they rapidly change in the international arena. The challenge of international organizations and their role in the global economy remains in the midst of the global economic governance approach, although it seemed utopian at first and regarded as too ambitious in redefining the international system.

A fundamental reorganization of the international system was not fair and everyone looks blown if this change will be unnoticed or will cause geopolitical pressures. In terms of prior work, it has been previously tried to emphasize the concepts already by known researchers in the field. The approach is a more theoretical one, with emphasis on results and future research.

The key results are related to some aspects of redefining the global economic governance in terms of international organizations. The implications are varied in terms of studying the concepts and address researchers in the field.

The main added value is the pragmatic approach of the role of international organizations and its formal relationship with the global economic governance.

Review of Literature

(i) Stiglitz in his book **'Globalization and Its Discontents'** has claimed that the IMF has mismanaged the globalization process for the least developed countries (LDCs). Driven by a "market fundamentalist ideology and special interests" ("global finance") in the advanced industrial countries, IMF officials have imposed the wrong policies on the LDCs and worsened their economic and political situations. He argues that the IMF's single-minded concerns about inflation and fiscal rectitude have been inappropriate for many countries and have neglected economic growth and employment. His solutions involve transparency and accountability and reducing the influence of special interests by giving conditions imposed by the IMF. **'Easterly's The Elusive Quest for Growth'** is another critical look at the institutions managing development and globalization.

(ii) Easterly, a former economist at the World Bank, criticizes the search for simple panaceas for development promoted by the Bank. "Neither aid nor investment nor population control nor adjustment lending nor debt forgiveness proved to be the panacea for growth." He documents how political and social factors (for example, corruption, ethnic conflict, inequality) in LDCs compound their economic problems rendering simple solutions ineffective. His corrective which must be vague, given his attacks on specific panaceas, is to make sure that all groups and incentives are properly structured to promote growth, including those of the international institutions like the World Bank.

(iii) Vreeland, a political scientist, in his book **'The IMF and Economic Development'** presents a social scientific analysis of the impact of IMF programs on growth in the LDCs. While many authors have presented such analyses before, only Vreeland has dealt with the major complicating factors that affect such programs. Using a formal and empirical model that accounts for both a government's decision to request an IMF loan and the IMF's decision to grant one, he shows that IMF programs do not promote growth. This result holds when compared with other countries not undergoing such programs, with the same country when it was not under such a program, and when selection bias for entry into the program is taken into account. Vreeland argues that countries often choose to undergo IMF reforms; they are not always forced to do so. Further, governments often choose to distribute the costs of such programs in ways that hurt poor groups, thus worsening inequality in addition to reducing growth. He blames the IMF for loaning to such countries and, like Stiglitz, for imposing conditions that prioritize controlling inflation and government spending. Like Stiglitz, he believes that the IMF should become more transparent, more attentive to the costs of its programs for labor and the poor, and more inclusive of the LDCs' concerns and priorities.

(iv) '**Lending Credibility**', by political scientist Randall Stone also finds fault with the IMF. But Stone is most concerned with the interference produced by the powerful advanced industrial countries, especially the United States. He shows that the IMF can only be successful in its mission to reduce inflation and find macroeconomic stability when powerful countries do not intervene to undermine the Fund's conditionality. Unlike Stigltiz and Vreeland, he argues that reducing inflation and deficits is and should be a priority, a position consistent with the IMF's own mission. Using a formal model to understand IMF interaction with LDC borrowers, he argues that in internationally powerful countries and ones that receive American support, IMF programs tend to fail because they are not credible. These countries receive loans but deviate more often from the IMF's conditions and thus fail to control inflation. Outside interference and politics undermine the IMF; its own policies are sound and effective. He focuses much on issues of compliance, while neglecting questions about why countries ask for loans in the first place. His book's strengths are thus Vreeland's weaknesses, and vice versa. Stone's solution is to push for greater IMF autonomy, almost the exact opposite of Stiglitz's and Vreeland's.

(v) '**World Poverty and Human Rights**' is a collection of essays written by a philosopher, Thomas Pogge. It combines normative and empirical analysis to argue that the developed countries and the international institutions they established are harming the poor countries and have an obligation to stop such harmful behavior. In the interdependent world we live in, the advanced industrial countries support an international system that makes coups, civil war and corruption in LDCs not only possible but likely. By upholding a government's privileges to borrow and assign rights for domestic resources no matter how bad the government is, the rich countries encourage a free for all for control of developing countries. Failure to recognize the rich nations' role in harming the poor countries depends on the "explanatory nationalism" that dominates current research and thinking. Pogge's main innovations are two. He argues that the resource and borrowing privileges conferred by the international system on the leaders of poor states constitute a causal link from rich countries, who maintain that system, to the misery of the poor. Normatively, his claims are innovative because they are founded upon his insistence on negative duties (do no harm) rather than positive ones (do well).

Pogge opines for a reform of global institutions so that they do no harm, or at least less. That these institutions leave the poor better off than a world without them is not enough for him; one must ask if institutions with better effects for the poor could feasibly be designed at little cost to the rich. His answer is in the affirmative, and he provides a number of interesting ideas, including a global fund for democracy, to help the poorest. Like the other authors, Pogge does not call for the dismantling of current international institutions; he calls for their reform and for changes in the behavior of developed countries running them.

Role of the International Economic Institutions

The roles of the three main institutions have changed over time; in addition, their membership has become nearly universal. All of these institutions were created by the victors in World War II and were intended to help them avoid another global depression. Part of the problem for these institutions lies in their legacy. They were designed to help the developed countries create a cooperative and stable world economy in a non-globalized world. The IMF was established to support the fixed exchange rate system created at the Bretton Woods Conference in 1944; its role was to aid countries that were experiencing difficulties in maintaining their fixed exchange rate by providing them with short term loans. It was a lender of last resort and a provider of funds in crisis, enabling countries to avoid competitive devaluations. Ensuring a stable international monetary system to promote trade and growth was its central mission. From an initial membership of 29 countries, it has become almost universal with 184 members.

With the collapse of the Bretton Woods fixed exchange rate system in the early 1970s, this role changed. The IMF dealt less with the developed countries and more with the developing ones. It provided long and short term loans at below-market interest rates for countries in varying degrees of economic difficulty, making it less distinct from the World Bank. It began attaching increasing numbers of conditions to those loans ("conditionality"), negotiating with countries to make major changes in their domestic policies and institutions. Promoting economic growth as well as resolving specific crises became its mission, which meant that ever more countries became involved in these so-called structural adjustment programs. Indeed, as Vreeland notes, in 2000 alone the IMF had programs with sixty countries, or more than one-third of the developing world. These changes made the IMF more similar to the World Bank. Formed after World War II, the Bank concentrated mostly on reconstruction and later on development; in 1960, with the formation of the International Development Association (IDA), the Bank moved further toward economic development programs. Many countries over the years have received both IMF and World Bank loans, often simultaneously. The World Bank also gives interest-free loans and grants (similar to foreign aid) to the poorest developing countries. This aid has been heavily used in Africa; indeed, in 2003, 51 percent of it went to sub-Saharan Africa. This overlap of missions, proliferation of adjustment loans, and expansion of conditionality are central issues today.

The WTO's central mission has been to promote trade liberalization by fostering negotiations among countries to reciprocally lower their trade barriers and providing information about countries' trade policies. Membership in the GATT/WTO has grown importantly over the years, from a mere 23 in 1947 to 146 countries in 2003. Like the IMF and World Bank, the GATT was originally a negotiating forum for the developed countries; its impact on the developing countries has grown slowly over time. The liberalization of trade policy has become an accepted doctrine for most developing countries; barriers in the developing world have fallen significantly since 1980. In addition, the WTO's mission has increasingly involved the connections between domestic policies and trade barriers. With significant lowering of tariffs and quotas, many domestic policies such as intellectual property laws, environmental policy, domestic subsidies, and tax laws, are now seen to affect trade flows and hence to reside within the WTO's jurisdiction. As with conditionality in the monetary domain, the attack on trade barriers has increasingly brought this international institution into contact with domestic politics. The GATT/WTO system has sponsored numerous trade negotiation rounds over the past fifty years. The most recently concluded negotiations, called the Uruguay Round, ended in late 1994 with the debut of the WTO and accords lowering trade barriers and extending agreements into other areas such as intellectual property and foreign investment. This system relies on reciprocity, attempting to balance countries' gains and losses. The WTO is now conducting the new Doha Round of trade negotiations, which is intended to address the problems of the developing countries more directly.

The Experience of the Developing Countries

Debate over these institutions has arisen from the seeming lack of progress in the developing world. Except for the World Bank, the original and primary mission of these institutions was not promoting growth in the developing world. Nevertheless, since the change in their roles from the 1970s onward, they have increasingly been judged by their impact on the poor. Fairly or not, the question has been whether these institutions have fostered development. Each of these institutions has promoted the adoption of market-friendly policies, and part of the reaction against them has been connected to these policies. "The widespread recourse of indebted developing countries to structural adjustment loans from the Bretton Woods institutions in the aftermath of the debt crisis of the early 1980s played a pivotal role in the redefinition of trade and industrialization strategies. Prominent among the conditions attached to these loans was the liberalization of policies towards trade and FDI (foreign direct investment). This was in line with the rising influence of pro-market economic doctrines during this period. Under these structural adjustment programs, there was a significant increase in the number of cases of trade and investment liberalization in many developing countries."

But concerns abound over whether trade and capital market liberalization, privatization, deregulation, austerity, and the other elements of the so-called "Washington Consensus" that these institutions advocated promote development in poor countries. If one looks solely at the economic side, progress has been mixed in many developing countries. As Easterly concludes, "there was much lending, little adjustment, and little growth in the 1980s and 1990s" in the developing world. Annual per capita growth for the developing countries averaged 0 percent for the years from 1980 to 1998, whereas from 1960–1979 their growth had averaged about 2.5 percent annually. Poverty remains very high with roughly 20 percent of the world's population living on less than a dollar a day and more than 45 percent on less than two dollars a day. Because of these conditions, some 18 million people a year die of easily preventable causes, many of them children. A sizable number of these countries were worse off economically in 2000 than they were in the 1980. World Bank data indicate, for instance, that per capita income was lower in 1999 in at least nine countries (for which data is available) than in 1960: Haiti, Nicaragua, Central African Republic, Chad, Ghana, Madagascar, Niger, Rwanda, and Zambia. From 1980 to 2002, twenty countries experienced a decrease in their human development indexes, which include more than just economic growth. Since 1980, the world's poorest countries have done worse economically than the richest. In the 1980s the high-income countries of the Organization for Economic Co-operation and Development (OECD) grew at 2.5 percent annually and in the 1990s at 1.8 percent; the developing countries grew at 0.7 percent and 1.7 percent, respectively. Moreover, if one excludes East Asia where the growth was extraordinary (5.6 percent in the 1980s and 6.4 percent in the 1990s), the developing countries grew much more slowly than the developed ones. Thus, they have been falling further behind the rich countries, increasing the gap between the two. As Lant Pritchett has shown, over the period of 1820 to 1992 the divergence in incomes between the world's rich and poor has grown enormously. In 1820, the richest country had three times the income that the poorest did; in the early 1990s this number was thirty. Much of this divergence is due to the rich countries' rapid growth.

Economic crises among the developing countries have also proliferated after the 1970s. In addition, the debt problems of many developing countries have increased. "Total debt of developing countries increased until 1999 and then stabilized at about $3 trillion as of last year that is, 2003. Furthermore, while debt has declined as a proportion of GDP, it remains high at some 40 percent, and the ratio of debt to exports at 113 percent. More importantly, the net resource transfers the resources available for use after paying interest has been negative in recent years for all regions. These magnitudes suggest that it is difficult to consider current levels of debt sustainable and helping growth." The performance of the developing countries has not been uniformly poor, however. From 1960 to 2000, life expectancy increased from 46 to 63 years in the developing world. Child mortality rates were halved in the same period, as were illiteracy rates. Poverty as a percentage of the developing countries' populations have declined recently including China, where the declines have been enormous, the percentage of people in the developing countries living on the poverty threshold of $1 a day has fallen from over 28 percent in 1990 to below 22 percent in 2000. The percentage living on $2 a day in the developing world also fell from 61 percent to 54 percent in this period. Unfortunately, the absolute numbers of the desperately poor have not fallen much, if at all, because of high population growth rates. The developing countries have also upgraded their role in the world economy.

They now are producers and exporters of manufactures and not primarily of primary products. In 2000, about 64 percent of low and middle income countries' exports were manufactures, while only 10 percent were agriculture, and their share of world trade in manufactures rose over this period from 9 percent to 26 percent. Especially in East and South Asia, the developing economies have become tightly integrated into the world production and trading system led by multinational corporations. This increase in the value-added and the diversification of developing countries' production and trade has been a boon for many.

This mixed record of economic outcomes has raised questions about the impact of these international economic institutions. But one must pose the counterfactual to assess their impact: would the performance of these countries have been better, the same or even worse had these institutions not existed?

Theories about the Functions and Benefits of International Institutions

Many international relations scholars have argued that countries should benefit from these institutions. States rationally decide to join them; therefore, they join only if the net benefits are greater than those offered by staying out of the organization. Membership is voluntary. The net utility derived from joining could be negative, but less negative than that incurred by remaining outside the institution. As Gruber has argued, if the most powerful states define the alternatives open to the developing countries and set up multilateral institutions, the developing countries can be better off by joining them than staying outside, but worse off than if the institutions never existed. The rush lately by all countries to join these institutions suggests that developing countries have found them to be more beneficial than the alternative of staying out, but it does not moot the question of whether they would be better off without any of these multilateral institutions in the first place. Four reasons are often theorized for the existence of these institutions: (1) constraining the great powers, (2) providing information and reducing transaction costs, (3) facilitating reciprocity, and (4) promoting reform in domestic politics.

Constraining the Great Powers

International institutions may exert a constraint on the underlying anarchy of the international system. They make the use of force and power by states to achieve their goals less likely; the rules, norms, and procedures established by these institutions replace to some extent the pursuit of national interest by power. Most importantly, as Ikenberry claims, they help to harness the behavior of the most powerful states. By creating and complying with these institutions, the Great Powers, or hegemony, can reassure other states that they will not take advantage of them. The strongest bind themselves to a set of norms and rules that the other states voluntarily agree to accept. Evidence for this effect is mixed. As the WTO points out, "trade is likely to expand and be more profitable under conditions of certainty and security as to the terms of market access and the rules of trade pre-commitment around a set of rules also diminishes the role of power and size in determining outcomes." This motivation is important in trade where countries with large markets, and hence market power, can use this to obtain more favorable trading arrangements in bilateral negotiations with smaller countries. Nevertheless, critics maintain that developing countries have not gained much from the GATT trade rounds; most of the gains have gone to developed countries. Some scholars even allege that the trade rounds have allowed the developed countries to exploit the developing ones by engaging them in unfair agreements. As Stiglitz says, "previous rounds of trade negotiations in the GATT/WTO had protected the interests of the advanced industrial countries or more accurately, special interests within those countries without concomitant benefit for the lesser developed countries." The unbalanced outcome of the recent Uruguay trade round is an important issue. "Several computable general equilibrium models have shown that the Uruguay Round results disproportionately benefit developed country gross domestic products (GDPs) compared to developing countries, and that some developing countries would actually suffer a net GDP loss from the Uruguay Round at least in the short run."

Developing countries have raised concerns about the equity of the outcome of this and other rounds. "With hindsight, many developing country governments perceived the outcome of the Uruguay Round to have been unbalanced. For most developing countries (some did gain), the crux of the unfavorable deal was the limited market access concessions they obtained from developed countries in exchange for the high costs they now realize they incurred in binding themselves to the new multilateral trade rules." Others note that asymmetric outcomes are an intrinsic part of the GATT/WTO bargaining process. "Trade rounds have been concluded through power-based bargaining that has yielded asymmetrical contracts favoring the interests of powerful states. The agenda-setting process (the formulation of proposals that are difficult to amend), which takes place between launch and conclusion, has been dominated by powerful states; the extent of that domination has depended upon the extent to which powerful countries have planned to use their power to conclude the round."

The counter factual one must pose is the following: without the GATT or WTO would the developing countries be better off if they had to negotiate bilaterally with the large, rich countries. Multilateralism seems well suited to giving the developing countries a better outcome than would such bilateral negotiations. "Multilateralism ensures transparency, and provides protection however inadequate against the asymmetries of power and influence in the international community." It may not only place some constraints on the behavior of the large, developed countries, but it may also encourage developing countries to realize their common interests and counterbalance the rich countries. By giving them more political voice than otherwise, institutions like the WTO may enhance their capacity to influence outcomes. Evidence of the constraining power of the IMF or World Bank is less apparent. Decisions in the IMF and World Bank are taken by weighted voting, with the rich countries and especially the United States having the majority share of votes. Since the end of the fixed exchange rate system in the early 1970s, these institutions have basically collected funds from the developed countries and private capital markets to give to the developing ones under increasing conditions. Conditionality has been designed by these institutions with the tacit support of the developed countries, and it has been negotiated with the poor ones. Since the late 1970s few, if any, developed countries have not been subject to IMF programs; only the developing world has. Article IV of the IMF charter requires surveillance of all members and discussion of the problems in their fiscal and monetary policies, but since the late 1970s, de facto this has not applied to the developed countries. The IMF has remarked on its own inefficacy: "Nowhere is the difficulty of conducting surveillance more apparent than in the relations between the IMF and the major industrial countries. Effective oversight over the policies of the largest countries is obviously essential if surveillance is to be uniform and symmetric across the membership, but progress in achieving that goal has been slow and hesitant." It is difficult to argue that the IMF and World Bank constrain the exercise of power by the developed countries. Indeed, these multilateral institutions may enhance the capacity of the rich countries to collectively enforce their will on the poor countries, as Rodrik argues.

Does their existence change the behavior of the rich? Without the two institutions, would the developed countries lend or donate as much as they do now. Does multilateral lending and aid substitute for or complement bilateral giving. Would the least well-off and the most politically insignificant countries be left to fend for themselves if they ran into economic crises, should the World Bank and IMF not exist? And would the terms of any aid or loans given bilaterally be worse for these countries than they are now. Evidence exists that bilateral aid tends to be more oriented toward the political and economic interests of donors than is multilateral aid. Some critics of the IMF and World Bank claim that countries would experience fewer crises since they would be more attentive to their financial situation in the absence of the moral hazard presented by the existence of these multilateral organizations. Others scholars have demonstrated that the distribution of aid and loans even with these institutions is weighted toward the economically better off and the politically more important developing countries. For instance, Stone shows that in lending to the transition countries the IMF gave more and imposed lighter conditions on those states with stronger political ties to the United States. Further, he shows how this political process undermines the credibility of the IMF's position and induces the recipient countries to ignore its conditionality. His research, however, does not really address the question of whether the IMF's presence affected the overall amount of lending or the allocation of those loans, relative to a situation where the Fund did not exist. These counterfactuals are essential for addressing questions about these multilateral institutions, but they are difficult to assess.

Providing information and reducing transaction costs

Following New Institutionalism theories, some argue that a major reason for these institutions is the lowering of transaction costs and the provision of information to facilitate multilateral cooperation in an anarchic world. As Keohane writes, international institutions "facilitate agreements by raising the anticipated costs of violating others' property rights, by altering transaction costs through clustering of issues, and by providing reliable information to members. They are relatively efficient institutions, compared to the alternative of having a myriad of unrelated agreements, since their principles, rules, and institutions create linkages among issues that give actors incentives to reach mutually beneficial agreements." For him, international institutions also reduce uncertainty by monitoring the member states' behavior and allowing decentralized enforcement through reciprocity strategies. Scholars such as Anne Krueger have suggested just such an informational role for the IMF and World Bank. Surveying and reporting on the policy behavior of member countries, providing information about the likelihood of crises, and being a repository of expert information are key roles for these institutions. The Meltzer Commission also emphasizes this role, and the most severe critics on the right imply that the IMF and World Bank should give up all roles except monitoring and providing expert information to member states. Others have noted the expertise role of the IFIs. "The World Bank is widely recognized to have exercised power over development policies far greater than its budget, as a percentage of North/South aid flows, would suggest because of the expertise it houses. This expertise, coupled with its claim to "neutrality" and its "apolitical" technocratic decision-making style, has given the World Bank an authoritative voice with which it has successfully dictated the content, direction, and scope of global development over the past fifty years."

The WTO has also been seen as an information provision institution. It monitors and reports on the compliance of states with the commitments they have made to each other. This task reassures other member countries and domestic publics about the behavior of their political leaders, making cooperation more likely and sustainable. Informational arguments suggest that all states gain from participation in such institutions. This mutual gain explains the voluntary participation of states in these multilateral forums. The expectation would be that developing countries join largely for these informational benefits, but there remains the issue of who provides what information for whose benefit. Are the developing countries providing more information than otherwise? Are the principal beneficiaries' private investors in the developing countries or in the developed world, other domestic groups, or the institutions themselves? Do the IMF and World Bank provide developing countries with useful information about other members or with expertise that would otherwise be unavailable? These empirical questions have not been examined much. One central complaint against the IMF and World Bank is that the policy advice they give (especially the "Washington Consensus" advice) has been unhelpful, if not detrimental, since it failed to take into account the circumstances of the developing countries. The claim is that the policy expertise given (or imposed via conditionality) has not been beneficial. For instance, Stiglitz, Bhagwati, and others have all criticized the IMF for pushing the developing countries into opening their capital markets. They have argued that little, if any, economic evidence or theory supports this, the consequences have been negative for most countries, and the main beneficiaries have been private investors in the developed world. As Stiglitz writes, "the main problem is that the IMF (and sometimes the other international economic organizations) presents as received doctrines propositions and policy recommendations for which there is not widespread agreement; indeed, in the case of capital market liberalization, there was scant evidence in support and a massive amount of evidence against." Even the advice to open their economies to trade has not been unquestioned. Economic analysis shows that the impact of trade openness on economic growth can be positive but also insignificant. Easterly's book is also an indictment of the economic policy prescriptions of the Bank and Fund. Each chapter shows how the prevailing wisdom guiding economic policy prescriptions in the IFIs has either been proven wrong or never been attempted to be proven right or wrong. As he concludes, "we saw that the search for a magic formula to turn poverty into prosperity failed. Growth failed to respond to any of these formulas." Vreeland's book supports these claims about the failed policy advice of the IMF. His research shows that IMF programs lower economic growth and redistribute income away from the neediest; the impact of conditionality is to retard development. As he concludes, this result means that either the IMF's policy prescriptions are incorrect or economic growth and poverty reduction are not the goals of the IMF. Stone's findings counter these; he shows that IMF programs do reduce influence and return greater macro-economic stability but only when they are not interfered with by political factors. Thus, even the informational value of the international institutions has been questioned.

Facilitating Reciprocity

International institutions facilitate reciprocity strategies among countries in an anarchic environment. Cooperation in anarchy relies on reciprocity, but more cooperation can be sustained if it need not require simultaneous and perfectly balanced exchanges. "International regimes can be thought of in part as arrangements that facilitate non-simultaneous exchange." Bagwell and Staiger have developed the most rigorous claims about the importance of reciprocity for the international trading system. If countries are sizable economic actors in world markets, then they can use trade policy to manipulate their terms of trade and gain advantages over their trading partners. If these big countries set trade policy unilaterally, they will arrive at an inefficient outcome, sacrificing the gains to be had from mutual trade liberalization. Reciprocity enhanced by the WTO's rules and monitoring can provide a context in which these big countries can achieve more efficient cooperative outcomes. The main function of international institutions is to make reciprocity credible and feasible. In the case of the large, rich countries in world trade this motivation seems apparent. The United States, European Union and Japan have used the GATT/WTO to enforce reciprocity strategies and lower their trade barriers. However, there is little evidence that this reciprocity has extended to the developing world. Many developing countries did not join the WTO until recently; most of the developing country members did not reciprocally liberalize their trade in the trade rounds.

> "In the period until the launch of the Uruguay Round and the formation of the WTO, only the industrial countries were meaningful participants in multilateral trade negotiations. They bargained amongst themselves to reduce trade barriers, while developing countries were largely out of this process and had few obligations to liberalize. The latter availed themselves of the benefits of industrial country liberalization, courtesy of the Most Favored Nation (MFN) principle, but that defined pretty much the limits of their contribution to or benefits from the General Agreement on Tariffs and Trade (GATT). Industrial countries were content with this arrangement, in part because it alleviated the pressure on them to liberalize sensitive sectors such as agriculture and clothing, but perhaps more importantly because the markets of developing countries were not at that stage sufficiently attractive."

This situation is not unexpected. Theories about the value of reciprocity in trade depend on the assumption that the country is a large trader (that is, it can affect prices); for most developing countries, this is not a realistic assumption. "Countries with small markets are just not attractive enough for larger trading partners to engage in meaningful reciprocity negotiations." The 100 largest developing countries (excluding the transition economies) accounted for 29 percent of total world exports in 2003; the United States alone accounted for 10 percent, the EU (excluding intra-EU trade) for 15 percent and Japan for 6.5 percent. In addition, many of the developing countries received preferential access to developed countries' markets. Ironically, this access has reduced their interest in reciprocal multilateral liberalization since it simply reduces their preference margins. The problem with granting preferential access in the goods trade as the payoff to small and poor countries is that it is counterproductive and even perverse. Although preferential access does provide rents in the short run, the empirical evidence suggests that preferences do not provide a basis for sustaining long-run growth. In addition, preferences create an incentive for recipients to have more protectionist regimes. For most of the developing world then, ensuring reciprocity has not been a main function of the trade regime.

Facilitating reform in domestic politics

Some scholars have speculated that joining an international institution and publicly agreeing to abide by its rules, norms, and practices has important domestic political consequences. It can help domestic leaders to alter policies at home that they otherwise would not be able to do. It can help them lock in "good" policies (that is, ones that enhance general welfare) and resist pressures by special interests to adopt "bad" policies (that is, ones that benefit special interests only). Or it can help domestic leaders to activate interest groups to counterbalance other groups' pressures and thus introduce different policies than otherwise. Several logics exist to support these claims. For some, once leaders join an institution it becomes hard for them to violate its practices since leaders who do so tarnish their international reputations and are less capable of making new agreements; their publics lose from this and are more likely to evict the leader, making non-compliance more costly than otherwise. Others argue that domestic publics receive signals from the monitoring of international institutions and that when the institution sounds a violation alarm, some domestic groups hear this and know their leaders are probably giving in to special interests and become more likely to vote them out of office. For others, the key is that achieving cooperative agreements with other countries brings advantages for some domestic groups that otherwise would not be involved in a change of policy; once their interests are engaged through the multilateral process, they can become strong proponents for policy change at home. Evidence for this binding effect is not extensive in the trade area.

Mattoo and Subramanian, for instance, show that the poorest countries (roughly a third of all countries) have not used the WTO to make commitments. "For a vast majority of the poor and small countries, both the proportion of tariff bindings in the industrial sector is small and the wedge between actual and committed tariffs is large, indicating that countries have given themselves a large margin of flexibility to reverse their trade policies without facing adverse consequences in the WTO."

Moreover, as others have noted, many of the developing countries chose to liberalize their trade regimes unilaterally. That is, they decided to open their markets before joining the WTO; membership in the WTO was not necessary for them to liberalize. Once they liberalized, however, membership then became more important; it helped to prevent the raising of trade barriers. The domestic political consequences of IMF and World Bank membership may be important but little research addresses this directly. Vreeland notes that countries underwent IMF programs out of choice as much as necessity. Governments were using the IMF to produce changes in policies that they desired, but unfortunately, these changes, did not produce economic growth or poverty reduction. His analysis demonstrates that the programs were used instead to promote the welfare of capital owners, who tend to be the richest groups in developing countries and thus may have further hurt developing countries. Stone's analysis also shows that compliance with the IMF has been variable, and that, especially for important borrowers, domestic binding or compliance has been low. In sum, we do not know what the overall domestic effect of IMF and World Bank membership on countries has been.

Four Sources of the Problems with International Institutions

If the WTO, IMF, and World Bank do not provide the beneficial for developing countries that scholars predict they might, what could explain this? Four claims have been advanced. Some argue that these institutions have minimal impact. Others argue that they are captured by either the powerful rich countries or by private producers and investors and so do not focus on the interests of the poor countries. Finally, the problems may lie with the internal organization and dynamics of the institutions themselves and the failure of the member countries to monitor their behavior.

(i) **No Impact**: It may be that these institutions had little or no impact on the developing countries. Their fate could be far more sensitive to other forces, such as globalization and domestic politics. Because of technological innovation, reduced communications and transportation costs, and policy changes, the developing countries have been increasingly exposed to the world economy. But the capacity of the IMF and World Bank has not grown proportionately, and thus, they are less able to help, especially at times of crisis. "The IFIs seek to fulfill their role of technical and financial support, but the relative size of their financing remains low. They constitute only about 19 per cent of total debt outstanding by developing countries, and only 13 per cent among middle-income countries." The developing countries have thus experienced increasing globalization while the IFIs capacity has not kept up with the rising demand for funds. The debate over the impact of globalization on the developing countries is too vast to join here, but suffice it to say that many scholars have argued that globalization is having a large effect on such countries (whether it is positive or negative is much debated). Globalization, however, is not disconnected from the WTO, World Bank, and IMF. These institutions were intended to help manage the process of integrating the developing economies into the world one. Nevertheless, the larger point is that globalization may have done more to affect these countries than these international institutions. Others have attributed the outcomes of the developing countries to their own domestic problems. Political instability, corruption, civil war, lack of the rule of law, and authoritarianism are viewed as the bigger sources of their problems. Recent research touting the importance of domestic political institutions supports this line of argument. Without institutions that protect private property rights for broad segments of the population, growth is unlikely. In this view, reforming domestic institutions is a financial priority to promote sustained growth. To the extent that the international institutions have advanced such institutional reform, they have helped the developing world. The degree of which they have permitted developing nations to avoid or postpone such domestic change, has hurt their prospects for development. From this perspective, it is essential not to attribute too much impact to the three international economic institutions. Much as realists in international relations maintain, these institutions may be more epiphenomenal; whatever impact they have, if any, is derived from their role in some larger political or economic structure.

(ii) **Capture by the Powerful Developed Countries**: For many scholars, Realists and others, these institutions were created by and for the interests of the large, rich countries. They were established at American initiative during its hegemony following World War II. American and European dominance in these organizations has been sealed by their sizable market power and their de facto control over the institutions' operations. Serving the interests of the advanced industrial nations has meant either that the interests of the poor countries were at best neglected. "There are thus serious problems with the current structure and processes of global governance. Foremost among these is the vast inequality in the power and capacity of different nation states. At the root of this is the inequality in the economic power of different nations. The industrialized countries have far higher per capita incomes, which translates into economic clout in negotiations to shape global governance. They are the source of much-needed markets, foreign investments, financial capital, and technology.

The ownership and control of these vital assets gives them immense economic power. This creates a built-in tendency for the process of global governance to be in the interests of powerful players, especially in rich nations." In this view, the international institutions have not helped much since they are oriented to promote the interests of the developed countries.

This bias operates in a number of ways in each organization. World Bank aid has been questioned. It has been heavily used in sub-Saharan Africa, but this region has done least well. Scholars have argued that this aid has been used to prop up authoritarian governments and to continue with failed policies longer than they otherwise could have. The link between the amount of aid a country received and its growth rate remains disputed; many find that aid alone has no significant impact on economic growth. But aid flows have not been allocated to the neediest countries. Studies show that donor interests, both economic and foreign policy ones, often dictate which countries receive what aid, and when. Countries with poor governments and policies may for other reasons receive large allocations of aid; the priorities of rich donors may undermine the developmental impact of aid.

According to other scholars, policy recommendations the developing countries were given reflected the experiences and interests of the rich countries. Trade liberalization promoted by the WTO and IMF occurred too quickly and without enough concern for financial alternative means for the poor countries to fund their budgets and develop social safety nets. For others, the problem is more how the agenda is set and how negotiating power is distributed. In the WTO, Steinberg shows the enormous power of the rich countries. "The secretariat's bias in favor of great powers has been largely a result of who staffs it and the shadow of power under which it works. From its founding until 1999, every GATT and WTO Director-General was from Canada, Europe, or the United States, and most of the senior staff of the GATT/WTO secretariat has been nationals of powerful countries. Secretariat officials' actions have usually been heavily influenced or even suggested by representatives of the most powerful states. For example, the package of proposals that became the basis for the final stages of negotiation in the Uruguay Round was largely a collection of proposals prepared by and developed and negotiated between the EC and the United States." IMF and World Bank conditionality programs mandating capital market liberalization, privatization and governmental austerity programs often ran a ground because the developing countries did not have the financial or legal institutions to support such policies. These policies might work in the context of the developed world where these institutions existed. An example of this is Russia, which Stiglitz and Stone discuss in detail. They show that American government officials pushed the IMF to loan and continue loaning large sums to Russia, that the IMF promoted policy changes that the Russian political economy could not handle, and finally that American pressure under-cut the ability of the IMF to induce Russia to reform. “The officials who applied Washington Consensus policies failed to appreciate the social context of the transition economies”; privatization in the absence of a legal framework of corporate governance only helped cause economic and political problems. Stone, who presents a more optimistic picture of the IMF largely because his central focus is on reducing inflation and not increasing growth or equality, shows that American influence on the IMF is pervasive and pernicious. In Russia’s case, for instance, he claims that the IMF made some mistakes (for example, in advising capital market liberalization in 1996, which was pushed by the Americans) but that most of the problems came not from IMF advice but from Russia’s failure to listen to the IMF. American pressure on the IMF and support for Russia were largely to blame for this outcome; Russian politicians knew that the IMF would never carry out their threats since the United States would never let them. Stone’s identification of the credibility problems that big country interference with the IMF engenders is a novel and subtle mechanism for rich country influence on the developing world.

Pressure from the rich countries has been seen as causing the international institutions at times to provide unhelpful advice as well as to shift the agenda and negotiating outcomes away from those favorable to the developing world. Bhagwati notes that “the rush to abandon controls on capital flows was hardly a consequence of finance ministers and other policy makers in the developing countries suddenly acknowledging the folly of their ways. It reflected instead external pressures from both the IMF and the U.S. Treasury”. Thacker shows that the United States exerts a great deal of influence over which countries get IMF loans. Countries voting similarly to the United States in the United Nations do better at the IMF. The literature on foreign aid also suggests that a country’s relationship to powerful sponsors makes a difference. Countries tend to get more aid from all sources the more ties they have to powerful, rich countries, especially the former colonial powers. Loans, aid, and advice may respond to the pressures of the most powerful developed countries, while trade agreements may promote the agendas and interests of these rich countries, but are these effects more or less likely when multilateral institutions exist than when these relations must be negotiated bilaterally?

(iii) **Capture by Private Producers and Investors**: Some have argued that the mission of the WTO, IMF, and World Bank has been increasingly dominated by the interests of private producers and investors. Sometimes their influence over these institutions operates through the power of the United States and European governments, and other times it operates independently or even at cross purposes from the developed countries' interests. The impression given is that these commercial and financial interests have hijacked the agenda of these institutions and have turned them into enforcers of open access to the markets of the poor countries. Furthermore, globalization has increased the influence of these private actors. The governance structure of the global financial system has also been transformed. As private financial flows have come to dwarf official flows, the role and influence of private actors such as banks, hedge funds, equity funds and rating agencies has increased substantially. As a result, these private financial agencies now exert tremendous power over the economic policies of developing countries, especially the emerging market economies.

Stiglitz claims that "financial interests have dominated the thinking at the IMF, and commercial interests have had an equally dominant role at the WTO." Even Bhagwati, who holds one of the most positive views about globalization, indicts the 'Wall Street-U. S Treasury complex" for many of the undesirable policies promoted by the international institutions and resultant problems they created for the developing countries. Is there strong evidence for this? One area that many scholars have pointed to is the WTO's promotion of trade-related aspects of intellectual property rights (TRIPs), especially in drugs and pharmaceuticals. As Bhagwati claims, "the multinationals have, through their interest-driven lobbying, helped set the rules in the world trading, intellectual property, aid and other regimes that are occasionally harmful to the interest of the poor countries." He notes that a key example of this harmful effect has been in intellectual property protection where "the pharmaceutical and software companies muscled their way into the WTO and turned it into a royalty-collection agency because the WTO can apply trade sanctions." He goes on to describe how the industries lobbied to get their views onto the American trade policy agenda and then used the United States government to force this onto the WTO and the developing countries.

The impact of private actors seems most well documented in the case of the IMF. Gould's research, for example, shows that the number and nature of conditionality in the IMF have responded increasingly to private investors. Their influence has grown because such investors play such a prominent role in international financing. As she claims, many of the controversial changes in the terms of Fund conditionality agreements reflect the interests and preferences of supplementary financiers. The Fund often provides only a fraction of the amount of financing that a borrowing country needs in order to balance its payments that year and implement the Fund's recommended program. Both the Fund and the borrower rely (often explicitly) on outside financing to supplement the Fund's financing. This reliance gives the supplementary financiers some leverage over the design of Fund programs. The supplementary financiers, in turn, want to influence the design of Fund programs because these programs help them ensure that borrowers are using their financing in the ways they prefer.

Perhaps international economic institutions like the IMF, World Bank, and WTO are a means for private actors to affect policies in the developing countries, particularly when globalization is high. Scholars "have pointed out that liberal international regimes improve the bargaining power of private investors' vis-à-vis governments and other groups in society." Again, the counterfactual deserves consideration: would the developing countries have been more or less subject to the pressure of private capital if these institutions had not existed.

(iv) **Internal Dysfunctions and Failure of Accountability**: Some scholars have been sensitive to the internal dynamics of the institutions themselves. They claim these organizations have developed their own internal logics, which may not serve the interests of the poor (or rich) countries. Effective control over them by either the advanced industrial countries or the developing ones may be difficult; long chains of delegation allow them much slack and make adequate monitoring of their behavior costly. Principal agent models suggest such outcomes are especially likely when multiple principals (that is, countries) try to control a single agent (that is, the institution); in these situations, the ability of the bureaucracy to play off different countries' interests and to avoid monitoring is maximized. Unlike the previous explanations that treated international institutions as mere servants of either powerful states or private producers and investors, this claim gives the organizations broad independence and wide latitude for autonomous action.

Vaubel has been one of the foremost proponents of this view. He produces evidence showing that bureaucratic incentives within the IMF and other international institutions lead to policies and practices inappropriate for their stated purposes. Concerns over career advancement and budget size induce actors within these agencies to focus on making loans and giving aid, but not on monitoring the results. Giving more loans and aid is always preferred to giving fewer, and recipients know this and use it to extract more. "If both institutions, that is, the IMF and World Bank are left to themselves, they will likely revert to internal bureaucratic politics determining loans. The act of making loans will be rewarded rather than the act of helping the poor in each country." As noted by Barnett and Finnemore, the IR literature has tended to take a benign view of international organizations, viewing them as instruments for facilitating cooperation and making efficient agreements. But "IOs often produce undesirable and even self-defeating outcomes repeatedly, without punishment much less dismantlement. In this view, decisions are not made after a rational decision process but rather through a competitive bargaining process over turf, budgets, and staff that may benefit parts of the organization at the expense of overall goals." For instance, they point to the case of the World Bank: "Many scholars and journalists, and even the current head of the World Bank, have noticed that the bank has accumulated a rather distinctive record of 'failures' but continues to operate with the same criteria and has shown a marked lack of interest in evaluating the effectiveness of its own projects." A series of internal problems could be responsible thus for the performance of these institutions vis-à-vis the developing countries. These four problems are not exclusive or exhaustive. Enumerating them is important. Figuring out which problems affect which institutions seems important and under-studied. Moreover, the type of reform desired depends on the problem. For example, Stone recommends further insulation of the IMF from the pressures of the donors, especially the United States. He wants the IMF to be more like an independent central bank. Insulation is desirable if the main problem is that they are too easily pressured by the rich countries or by private investors. Stiglitz, among others, however, has the opposite view. He thinks they should be more transparent and open to developing-country influence. Studies of bureaucracy in general see insulation as necessary, if undesirable, outside influences are strong and leaders are tempted to yield to them; but they see insulation as the problem itself if the bureaucracy's unaccountability and standard operating procedures are the failings. If the IMF's problem results mainly from its own internal organization and logic, then further insulation is only going to worsen the problem. Without further systematic evidence about the sources of these institutions' main problems in delivering benefits to the developing countries, reform proposals may do more harm than good.

In sum, today's international economic institutions seem to be falling short of the goals that theories expect of them, and the reasons seem numerous.

The current state of our knowledge does not warrant advocating the abolition of these international institutions, however. They appear to provide some benefits to the poor countries over the most likely counterfactual scenarios. But they probably could be reformed to provide even greater benefits.

CHAPTER IV

INTERNATIONAL JUSTICE AND INSTITUTIONS: NORMATIVE PERSPECTIVES

Empirical assessments of the impact of international institutions on the developing countries provide a baseline for discussion of the role that these institutions should play. It bears a moment to ask about the normative side of this question: should, and to what extent should, these institutions be responsible for addressing the interests of the developing world. Discussions of international distributive justice have multiplied lately as globalization has spread and the divergence between the fortunes of the rich and poor seems to have grown.

Rawls has famously argued that distributive justice (and especially his difference principle) does not apply globally; it only extends domestically to "well-ordered" societies. As Nagel claims, "the ideal of a just world for Rawls would have to be the ideal of a world of internally just states." For "burdened societies," which include most of the developing world, the well-ordered countries have only a "duty of assistance." The meaning of this duty is not clear, but it is not a claim to distributive justice. For Rawls, the main problem of burdened societies is not wealth or resources; it is their political and social culture. The duty of assistance seems to call most for improving the observation of human rights in these countries and not in rectifying their economic policies or reducing inequalities. Furthermore, once the world's poor have become free and equal citizens within a reasonably liberal society, this duty is fulfilled; it does not require that countries reach a certain standard of living or a low level of inequality.

Since promoting human rights and creating well-ordered liberal societies have not been central missions of these three international institutions, it is unclear how Rawls would judge them. Although he recognizes the existence of negotiated international arrangements governing matters such as trade and finance, Rawls pays very little attention to the extent of their influence in the economic and political lives of domestic societies, and does not seriously consider the extent to which they constitute a phenomenon at the international level analogous to that of the "basic structure" of domestic societies.

In contrast, the cosmopolitan perspective on global justice makes three important points. First, distributive justice must be conceived globally, not just nationally. Second, the counterfactual assessment of these institutions used in empirical analysis is not sufficient to evaluate their performance on global distributive justice grounds. Third, because of these claims, research into development and international institutions must be changed.

Distributive Justice Is Global

The first claim of the cosmopolitan view is that distributive justice must be conceived on a global level, not just a national one; it is universal. Theory and factual conditions lead to this position. Rejecting Rawls and other "nationalist" theories, theorists of global justice argue that no consistent logical argument can be sustained that limits justice to the domestic sphere. Barry's notion of justice as impartiality is a main foundation for this view. But Pogge also advances the power of moral universalism.

He claims that "Rawls runs afoul of moral universalism since he fails to meet the burden of showing that his applying different moral principles to national and global institutional schemes does not amount to arbitrary discrimination in favor of affluent societies and against the global poor." Using Rawls' own idea of the "basic structure," Buchanan in a recent critique shows that a global basic structure exists, which is composed of "regional and international economic agreements (including General Agreement on Tariffs and Trade, North American Free Trade Agreement, and various European Union treaties), international financial regimes (including the International Monetary Fund, the World Bank, and various treaties governing currency exchange mechanisms), an increasingly global system of private property rights, including intellectual property rights that are of growing importance as technology spreads across the globe, and a set of international and regional legal institutions and agencies that play an important role in determining the character of all of the preceding elements of the global basic structure." If this structure exists, then "like a domestic basic structure, the global basic structure in part determines the prospects not only of individuals but of groups, including peoples in Rawls's sense. It is therefore unjustifiable to ignore the global basic structure in a moral theory of international law to proceed either as if societies are economically self-sufficient and distributionally autonomous or as if whatever distributional effects the global structure has are equitable and hence not in need of being addressed by a theory of international distributive justice." Theoretically, moral universalism and justice as impartiality both imply that theories of domestic justice have global reach. Other theorists make this argument by relying on factual claims. Globalization itself creates the need for a global theory of justice. The increasing integration of national economies into a global one means that all countries are increasingly affected by what goes on in the others. We are now "one world" to use Peter Singer's phrase; gone are the days of the Westphalian system of individual states. States are not separate, self-contained units that can implement autonomously their own principles of justice; their internal situation is affected by international factors. "These institutional interconnections an important aspect of globalization render obsolete the idea that countries can peacefully disagree about justice, each committing itself to a conception of justice appropriate to its history, culture, etc. In the contemporary world, human lives are profoundly affected by non-domestic social institutions by global rules of governance, trade and diplomacy, for instance in light of these changed circumstances, then we must aspire to a single, universal criterion of justice which all persons and peoples can accept as the basis for moral judgments about the global order." Furthermore, the argument that the advanced, industrial countries are not responsible for the developing countries' problems because these problems were caused by factors internal to the developing nations is untenable in such a world. As Beitz says, "it is not even clear that the question about the relative importance of domestic versus international causes of development is intelligible as it arises for contemporary developing societies which are enmeshed in the global division of labor: a society's integration into the world economy, reflected in its trade relations, dependence on foreign capital markets, and vulnerability to the policies of international financial institutions can have deep and lasting consequences for the domestic economic and political structure. Under these circumstances, it may not even be possible to distinguish between domestic and international influence on a society's economic condition."

Pogge goes further and shows in two specific ways how the international system directly affects economic and political outcomes in the developing world. He identifies the 'international resource privilege' and the 'international borrowing privilege' as critical forces in shaping developing countries, furthermore, he shows that they are sustained by the current global system and the developed countries' interests in that system. These forces harm the developing countries, and the rich countries are responsible for these privileges.

Pogge proceeds in three steps. In the current international system, any group that controls the preponderance of the means of coercion in a country is internationally recognized as the legitimate government, no matter how it came to power, how it exercises power or whom it represents. Once recognized, this government has the legal power to confer domestic and global ownership rights to all of the country's resources. It possesses the right to sell the country's resources and to borrow money for whatever purposes it decides. Given this situation, all domestic groups are thereby encouraged to lay claim to the leadership of a country, thus providing powerful incentives toward coups and civil wars. These privileges often mean that a country's resources are sold off and it borrows heavily to the benefit of a few individuals and the long-term detriment of the public. As Pogge claims, these "two aspects of the global economic order, imposed by the wealthy societies and cherished also by the authoritarian rulers and corrupt elites in the poorer countries, contribute substantially to the persistence of severe poverty. These global factors thereby strongly affect the overall incidence of oppression and poverty and also, through their greater impact on the resource-rich countries, international differentials in oppression and poverty." The advanced industrial countries and the international institutions they set up are then responsible not only because they maintain the current international system and its rules but also because they freely buy the goods sold by such corrupt and unelected governments and offer them loans. Thus for theoretical and empirical reasons, distributive justice must be cosmopolitan in scope; and the role of international institutions must be scrutinized from such a moral perspective.

Rawls and his defenders do not accept this position. While space does not permit recapitulating the debate, they have made two strong counter arguments. They maintain that the principles of justice do not extend across people. A central part of their argument is that states are valuable. Justice is relevant only within states because individuals within them consent to be governed by certain principles and agree to be coerced, if need be, into doing so. The individualistic perspective of cosmopolitanism is wrong; it greatly "underrates the moral significance of political communities." As Rawls says, "an important role for government, however arbitrary a society's boundaries may appear from a historical point of view, is to be the effective agent of a people as they take responsibility for their territory and the size of their population, as well as for maintaining the land's environmental integrity." Not only this, in well-ordered societies self-government creates and depends on "common sympathies" and strong reciprocal moral obligations. "Citizens have powerful obligations of mutual concern and respect to one another because the political institutions for which they are all responsible determine patterns of opportunities and rewards for all." Justice in this perspective is relevant only domestically.

As a second point, they maintain that domestic factors, not international ones, are the source of the plight of the developing countries. Domestic defects have prevented some of the developing countries from moving forward, and these domestic problems are unrelated to the rich countries. The rich countries have neither caused harm in the developing ones, nor can they rectify problems in the poor countries. There is no basic structure that links the fates of the developed and developing nations. If one accepts the position of the Rawlsians and "nationalists", then the next two points are irrelevant; the only obligation of the international institutions is the duty of assistance.

Current Counterfactual Assessments are Insufficient

Any other element of cosmopolitan normative argument concerns the evaluation of the IMF, World Bank and WTO. Above all, the institutions were evaluated on the basis of the counterfactuals that arise from comparison cross-nationally and longitudinally. Did these institutions leave the developing countries better off than they would have been in a world without their presence? Pogge and Singer, among others, reject this standard of evaluation (for slightly different reasons). For them, a positive answer to this counter-factual is not sufficient to conclude that the present international system is a moral one. For them, another question must be asked: could one design another international system or reform the current international institutions so as to provide greater benefits for the poor countries at very low cost to the developed countries. This moral standard follows that proposed by Singer more than thirty years ago. Singer's "two conclusions then were the strong one that affluent people's not contributing money or time to voluntary international aid agencies is immoral, in the same way that a bystander's failing to save a drowning child would be immoral, and the stronger one that non contribution to such agencies only ceases to be wrong when one has reduced oneself to a level such that any further sacrifice would actually be worse for those whom one is trying to help." The right standard for judging these institutions are whether reforms in them could be easily made that would provide greater benefits for the poor at minimal cost to the rich. For Singer, the rich countries have a positive duty to help the poor and one that is very extensive.

For Pogge, the counterfactual is similar but his case rests on the negative duty that the rich countries are obligated to stop taking actions that hurt the poor. This normative case again rests on empirical evidence. As noted above, poverty and inequality globally remain widespread, and in some views they are increasing. Furthermore, as noted above, the wealthiest countries have been getting wealthier and often doing so even faster than the poor ones. This means that the rich countries have even more resources with which to help the poor, and the poor because they are so poor can be helped easily. The poorest 2.8 billion people, or 46 percent of human kind, have 1.2 percent of aggregate world income now; the richest countries with 900 million in population have almost 80 percent of world income. Achieving the UN Millennium Summit goals, which include halving the number living on $1 a day or less, would cost about $40–60 billion a year in extra aid, which is less than 1 percent of the rich countries' total annual income. Hence, he claims that for very little the rich countries could dramatically help the poor, and thus concludes that the current international order requires reform.

For the international institutions, the issue is whether they could be changed in ways that would improve the lives of the absolute poor without much impact on the developed countries. Pogge, Singer, Beitz, and others claim the answer is in the affirmative. "What matters for a moral economic assessment of an economic order under which many are starving is whether there is a feasible institutional alternative under which such starvation would not occur." These scholars do not see the counterfactual used in empirical analysis as morally compelling. "Suppose poverty and poverty deaths are actually less now than they would be if the WTO had not been concluded. It is tempting to infer that the new regime is then beneficial to the poor, since it treats them better than the old one would have done. But this reasoning fails by unjustifiably taking the continuation of the old regime as the neutral baseline."

The problem lies not with the developing countries for accepting the WTO, since they have little choice, but with the WTO and the developed countries for crafting the regime so that it does not help the poor more. The developed countries could have negotiated a different WTO agreement, one fairer to the poor with little cost to themselves. "Perhaps even more millions who would have died from poverty-related causes had the WTO regime not existed have in fact survived with the WTO in place. Governments in the rich countries cannot use this benefit to justify the harm they caused, because they could have avoided most of this harm, without losing the benefit, by making the WTO treaty less burdensome on the developing countries. They did not do this because they sought to maximize their gains from the agreement." Relinquishing a small portion of their gains, he claims, the developed countries at low cost could have fashioned a WTO providing many more benefits to the poor. The same is said to be true for the IMF and World Bank, where if the developed countries and the institutions themselves did not bargain for maximum advantage, the developing countries could do better. The proliferation of conditionality that Gould documents in the IMF is one example, and the imposition of austerity by the IMF leading to slow or negative growth and rising domestic inequality that Vreeland documents is another. Furthermore, refusing to give aid to or loan to governments that come to power through coups or other non-democratic means might alleviate the problems generated by the international resource and borrowing privileges. As Pogge concludes, "our present global economic order produces a stable pattern of widespread malnutrition and starvation among the poor, with some 18 million persons dying each year from poverty-related causes, and there are likely to be feasible alternative regimes that would not produce such similarly severe deprivations." In arriving at a normative assessment of the IMF, World Bank, and WTO, Pogge among others claims that one might need to use a standard of moral judgment that is different from the usual counterfactual that scholars employ in positive analysis.

The "Nationalist" Research Agenda Must Change

Pogge labels much of the current research on the developing countries as "nationalist." He argues that there is a research bias in the field such that domestic and local factors are more likely to be identified as causes of poverty and underdevelopment than global ones. "That research into poverty turns up national or local factors is due not the world but to how these inquiries are focused: on the differential evolution of poverty in various developing countries and regions. It would be an analogous mistake to conclude, from the fact that comparative poverty research uncovers national and local factors, that the existing global economic order is a not a causal contributor to poverty." Pogge thus criticizes this "explanatory nationalism" and calls for more research into the global sources of poverty. Comparative research into poverty and growth should thus include international variables. For instance, economists and political scientists have run many growth regressions, based largely on economic models and including mainly national level variables. Pogge's recommendation would be to add international variables like the participation of countries in the WTO, IMF, or World Bank and their programs. He would applaud Vreeland's research, while calling for an even broader approach. He recognizes that many of these international factors are constant; the international resource privilege has existed since the Treaty of Westphalia (1648), for example. But the interaction of such factors with national-level ones that vary can increase one's leverage on these problems. "Corruption in Nigeria is not just a local phenomenon rooted in tribal culture and traditions, but encouraged and sustained by the international resource privilege. This correlation has a 'nationalist' explanation: national resource abundance causes bad government and flawed institutions by encouraging coups and civil wars. But this nationalist explanation crucially relies on a global background factor, the international resource privilege, without which a poor country's generous resource endowment would not handicap its progress toward democratic government and economic growth." His research advice is not just to add or take account of international factors but also to examine them in interaction with domestic ones. Maybe the impact of resource endowments on growth depends on the existence of the international resource privilege. When these international factors vary either over time or across countries, their inclusion and interaction with domestic factors is good advice. After all, in this globalized world, conducting research on countries integrated into the global system without taking account of those global linkages is a strategy that can mislead. His research advice is simple and feasible in many cases: avoid the "explanatory nationalist" bias by including international variables and their interactions with domestic ones in order to properly assess the sources of poverty and development.

What Is to Be Done

What does one know about the impact of the major international economic institutions, the IMF, World Bank, and the WTO, on the developing countries? Have these institutions improved the lives of the poor in these countries. Have they made the developing countries better off than they would have been in the absence of these global institutions? Is this counterfactual the appropriate standard to evaluate them? What is the moral obligation of the rich countries and their international institutions to the poor ones? Should the institutions be reformed to better fulfill their "duty of assistance" to the poor? Or is a better standard for their evaluation one that asks whether the institutions could be reformed at low cost to the rich countries so that they would provide more beneficial to the poor ones. How do normative and positive analyses together shed light on these institutions?

In terms of the four major functions that theories of international institutions identify, these three global institutions seem to have failed to live up to the expectations of these theories in their impact on the developing countries. They have had a difficult time constraining the large, developed countries; most of the time these countries have bargained hard to maximize their advantage vis-à-vis the developing nations. Perhaps they have left the developing countries better off than if they had to negotiate bilaterally for access to trade, aid, and loans, but it seems as if these institutions could have bargained less hard with the developing countries at little cost to themselves or the developed countries and thus provided more benefits for the poor. The IMF, World Bank, and WTO have certainly helped provide monitoring and information. But the monitoring and information provision have been asymmetric; it is the developing countries that are monitored and provide more information than otherwise. This action, however, may make the developed countries and private investors more likely to trade with, invest in, and provide loans to the poor countries, but the terms of these agreements have often imposed multiple and powerful conditions on the developing countries that may have impeded their growth. Facilitating reciprocity has been a central function attributed to international institutions. For these three organizations, reciprocity vis-à-vis the developing world has not been a central mission; trade agreements have often been very asymmetric and the aid and lending programs are one way. Finally, the ability to alter domestic politics by creating support or locking it in for reform has been less studied, but seems to clearly have had an impact. The impact of the international institutions on the developing countries and their domestic situation has been powerful but not always benign.

The difficulties faced by the international institutions in providing benefits for the developing countries have arisen from at least four sources. It may be the case that globalization has simply overwhelmed these institutions and that their impact is minor compared to other factors, especially with a large and open world economy, and it is likely that domestic weaknesses account for part of their poor performance. But their problems may also lie in the pressures exerted by the large, developed countries and private producers and investors. Both of these groups have shaped the functioning of the WTO, IMF, and World Bank. The powerful, rich countries have bargained hard within these institutions to advance their own interests. Private producers and investors have directly and indirectly affected the performance of the institutions through their central role in the world economy. All of these institutions were established to support and facilitate private trade and capital flows, not to supplant them. Finally, one cannot overlook the claim that part of the problems arises from the internal organization and procedures of the institutions themselves. Making loans and imposing conditions may be more important for career advancement than measuring the impact of these activities on the developing nations.

Positive, empirical research asks the question of whether the developing world would have been better or worse off with the presence of these international institutions than without them. The evidence suggests that even though problems abound with the institutions, one cannot rule out the counterfactual: without these institutions many developing countries could be worse off as they faced bilateral negotiations with the most powerful countries. Thus, advocating their abolition is premature. Nevertheless, one has to ask if this question is the right one. Arguments from one stream of moral philosophers imply that it is not. Cosmopolitan versions of global distributive justice see this question as insufficient. They propose one ask whether these institutions could be reformed at low cost to the wealthy countries to provide more benefits to the poor. Are these institutions the most feasible ones that could help the developing countries without imposing large costs on the developed ones?

By many accounts, the answer is negative. A number of feasible and low cost reforms could be enacted that would render these institutions much more helpful to the poor at limited cost to the rich. Pogge makes such a case for the WTO. By the standards posed in global distributive justice arguments, reforming the international institutions is imperative. Interestingly, normative and positive analyses sometimes agree; some international economists such as Bhagwati and Stiglitz propose similar reforms.

In addition to policy implications, several ramifications for future research arise from the arguments surveyed here. Pogge's point about the "nationalist" research agenda in the field is salient. His prescription that we include more international factors in research on the sources of poverty and economic and political development is not unfamiliar and seems a worthy one. Including global factors and their interactions with domestic ones in comparative studies is an important step that cannot be emphasized enough.

The final would benefit from more research on the actual effects of international institutions, rather than debates about whether they are autonomous agents. More empirical research on the ways in which these institutions function and on the forces that prevent them from functioning as our theories predict is essential. This is particularly the case vis-à-vis the developing countries, many of whom do not have the capacity to evaluate the impact of these institutions on their fortunes. "Identifying who gains and who loses from existing policies is important both to determine the need for policy change and to build support for such change. For example, documenting how specific OECD policies hurt the poor both at home and in developing countries can have a powerful effect on mobilizing support for welfare improving reforms. Building coalitions with NGOs and other groups that care about development is vital in generating the political momentum that is needed to improve access in sensitive sectors and improve the rules of the game in the WTO." Generating greater academic knowledge thus may contribute vastly to producing better policy and outcomes, which may be a moral imperative given the grave problems of the developing countries.

Counterfactuals are defined as "subjunctive conditionals in which the antecedent is known to be false" (Tetlock and Belkin 1996, 4). A critical issue is how can one know what would have happened if the antecedent was false, that is, if factor X, which was present, had not been present. This problem of co tenability, identified by Elster (1978) early on, remains crucial: counterfactuals require connecting principles that sustain but do not require the conditional claim, and these connecting principles must specify all else that would have to be true for the false conditional claim to have been true.

CHAPTER V

GLOBAL GOVERNANCE REFORMS

The Central Challenge: The Mismatch of Global Institutions and Global Challenges

The central challenge of the 21st century is that the institutional framework for dealing with contemporary global challenges does not match the scope, scale and nature of the challenges themselves. If the 20th century represented the culmination of a long history of the nation-state as the institutional framework capable of addressing the challenge of modernity, the global challenges of the 21st century seem to exceed the grasp of the current international institutional framework. This conundrum does not mean that the nation-state needs to be superseded by a better and stronger set of international institutions. To the contrary, the nation-state and national political leaders constitute the foundation of political legitimacy necessary for global governance and international institutional reform to move forward.

There are several specific manifestations of institutional inadequacy that are currently under scrutiny and which have generated proposals for reform. As comprehensive and important as these four manifestations of incongruence are, they do not represent the full nature of the mismatch but only illustrate several obvious gaps in adequacy. First, the United Nations Security Council as a creation of the post-World War II alliance in 1945 is confronting a crisis of obsolescence. Not only are Germany and Japan, the second and third largest economies in the world, not represented as permanent members of the Security Council, but, with the important exception of China, there are no developing countries represented either. Second, since the WTO meetings in Seattle in 1999, there is a growing demand for changes the voting shares in the Bretton Woods Institutions (the World Bank and the International Monetary Fund) to better reflect current realities. Third, embedded in these reform issues but beyond them is the growing reality and tension concerning the unipolar nature of the military, economic, media, and political power of the United States in its conduct of foreign policy. Fourth, global challenges in the global age seem to be characterized more by interconnectedness rather than by isolation. This throws an international system based on "specialized agencies" into a state of inadequacy as the nature of contemporary interconnected problems exceeds their expertise based on specialization.

These four challenges are sufficient by themselves to justify a strong push toward international institutional reform, even if there were not more to the story. Yet, reform on all four fronts is severely circumscribed by practical political constraints. What seems to be needed to break the deadlock and move forward are several conceptual innovations that together can reframe the discussion and possibly provide some daylight in an otherwise gloomy set of prospects for global governance reform. What follows is an effort to create a set of categories for thinking about reform which attempt to contain the tensions and trade-offs involved in achieving reform rather than try to avoid them.

It should be said at the outset that if the institutional framework today is inadequate, it does not mean that it is possible to invent a new formulation that is fully adequate and achieves unblemished enhancements on all fronts. The world is an imperfect and messy place. And any proposal of global reform will fall short of the ideals for democracy, equity, and justice for all.

Concepts and Categories for Framing Problems and Approaches

Specialization versus Integration

If global governance reforms are necessary in order to adequately address the challenges of the 21st century, the issue of the "adequacy" of the nation-state as a unit of representativeness, agency and legitimacy in the global age could easily be questioned. Many have argued that the increasing globalization of finance, trade, migration, and media have weakened nation-states and their capacities to manage domestic affairs. But the fundamentals of globalization do not seem to be juxtaposed to the nation-state so much as they are to the Western notion of modernity.

One way to look at this is to realize that the 20th century was based on the Western notion of progress rooted in the universality of human knowledge derived from specialization in disciplines and problem areas. Western modernism for much of the 20th century was understood in the West especially as a universal form of modernism which would be shared by all humanity as progress spread. To be characterized by a fundamentally different construct, 21st century is already being seen as posing challenges distinct from the 20th century. The challenges of this century seem to be ones which require understanding the inter-linkages between challenges and the interfaces between them rather than only burrowing deeper within the problem area itself as the primary means of developing approaches.

While the 20th century relied on specialists, the 21st century may come to rely more on people who are integrationists, capable within their expertise but excelling in their grasp of the relationship between their area of expertise and those adjacent to its which increasingly drive results within it. As noted biologist Edward O. Wilson has written: “Most of the issues that vex humanity daily ethnic conflict, arms escalation, over-population, abortion, environment, endemic poverty, to cite several most persistently before us cannot be solved without integrating knowledge from the natural sciences with that of the social sciences and humanities.” (Wilson (1998) page 13.) The linkages among challenges and between disciplines and approaches are fundamental drivers of institutional inadequacy and mismatch.

Distinction between Institutions and Governance

There is a fundamental distinction between the configuration of international institutions and the process for global governance. In the debate on global reform, there seems to be confusion between reform in the institutional arrangements and governance reform, as if they were the same when in fact they are related but separate issues. The adequacy of the current configuration of international institutions to confront global problems is a separate issue from that of global governance. One is an issue of structure and framework; the other is one of process and dynamics.

Distinction between Representativeness Legitimacy and Performance Legitimacy

It is useful to distinguish between performance legitimacy and representativeness legitimacy. What is not always clear is that there is a trade-off, or at a minimum a tension, between these two. For example, the UN General Assembly must represent the high water mark for representativeness legitimacy among all international institutions because it is based on the one country-one vote principle. And yet it is not clear that it is the best vehicle for “getting things done”. The G-7/8 summit mechanism, by contrast, could be an efficient forum for decision-making because there is a small number of leaders present enhancing performance legitimacy. However, representativeness legitimacy is increasingly questioned since the G-7/8 countries constitute a group of Western, industrial countries with less than 15 percent of the world's population in a world that is increasingly non-Western and non-industrial.

Authority, Agency and Political Legitimacy in Global Governance

For global governance reform to sufficiently enhance legitimacy, it is not enough to generate greater performance legitimacy alone through greater efficacy nor is it enough that reforms embody only greater representativeness legitimacy. Political legitimacy is the perception that authorities with capacities to execute decisions (agency) derive their authority from a foundational idea rooted in widely shared values. Authorities can gain political legitimacy by political processes, by being elected, for example, or by reflecting the values, interests and goals of their people even if they do not formally represent them. This last source of political legitimacy can be seen as being honored in the breach with recent examples of leaders who cease to reflect their peoples' values, interests and goals being run off as leaders: Marcos; Pinochet; etc.

There are also broader processes involved in how leaders can achieve legitimacy by reflecting the broad aspirations of people that embody common values but go beyond narrow interests by articulating broader but specific goals which can be addressed and even achieved by agency, process and institutions. Specific goals have the advantage of laying out expectations of specific results for which quantitative indicators can be created. By monitoring the evolution of critical indicators and evaluating specific results, the political interaction of leadership, decision processes (agency articulation) and institutions can become transparent and accountable which enhances the legitimacy of the entire undertaking, even if progress is not as high as anticipated. The openness, inclusiveness and integrity of the process reinforce legitimacy beyond that derived from the values-aspirations-consensus-goal formation sequence. This entire process enhances democratic accountability.

For all these reasons, national leaders tend to embody political legitimacy. Whether through formal political processes or through informal consensus articulation modalities, national leaders seem to be perceived as highly legitimate vehicles for agency. While perhaps not always the ideal embodiment of democracy, it is nonetheless difficult to find alternatives which can supersede them. Nonetheless, it is necessary to create safeguards, incentives and assurances around national political leaders to ensure accountability, integrity and legitimacy. It is not an easy exercise to construct alternative general rationales to justify that leaders other than national leaders be able to trump national political leaders in constituting legitimate agents for the will of national societies. Therefore, summits consisting of national political leaders have greater authority, agency and legitimacy for taking decisions than alternative leaders might. As Robert Keohane has written recently: "the relevant question is whether, in light of feasible alternatives, existing or attainable forms of multilateralism are legitimate relative to these alternatives. They can only be defended on the basis of comparative legitimacy: the normative superiority of partial reliance on them for authorization of action, over other feasible processes." (Keohane (2005), pp 18 and 22).

The issue of who decides on the future of the institutional configuration is an issue of global governance by accountable national political leaders, as well. The role of the United Nations is not to govern but to provide a forum for decisions. Even though the Bretton Woods agencies, for example, or the WTO and the WHO are all UN agencies, it is not for the UN Secretary General or the UN Secretariat or the heads of the UN agencies among themselves (through the Chief Executive Board) to sort out the foundational issue of institutional configuration. It is a global governance issue requiring strategic guidance by political leaders.

There is at the moment no locus of authority, agency or legitimacy to provide overall strategic guidance for defining the inter-institutional arrangements that are needed for the future. Inter-institutional relations decisions are by nature not for institutional heads to determine; the international institutions are accountable to national governments so that it is necessary that national leaders in a political setting provide guidance, oversight and accountability regarding inter-institutional relations. The current void at the apex is a major reason for the mismatch between the international institutional framework and 21st century global challenges.

The Global Age and Global Challenges

Frameworks and Goals for the Global Age

What is really quite stunning is that despite the fact that the configuration of international institutions and global governance processes are seen to be inadequate to address global challenges, this inadequacy has not prevented there being generated two universally endorsed frameworks for prioritizing global issues and setting goals for dealing with them: the Millennium Declaration and the Millennium Development Goals (MDGs). Both derive from a sequence of UN conferences in the early to mid 1990s which generated a plethora of recommendations for action on children (Jomtien 1990), environment (Rio 1992), human rights (Vienna 1993), population (Cairo 1994), social development (Copenhagen 1995), and women (Beijing 1995). These world conferences led to a prioritization of seven International Development Goals (IDGs) by national authorities, development cooperation ministers of industrial countries, in May 1996 focusing on poverty, gender equality, and education, health, and environment goals to be achieved by 2015. (DAC 1996)

Millennium Summit at the UN General Assembly in New York in September of 2000 heads of state and governments promulgated a "Millennium Declaration" which has five fields of action: security, human rights, democracy and governance, poverty and development, and environment. The Millennium Declaration is a framework for action on global issues for all actors the private sector, civil society, national governments and international institutions in both industrial and developing countries, authorized by national leaders. The MDGs are a set of specific goals and quantitative targets and indicators which provide benchmarks for efforts and results achieved in addressing the multidimensional aspects of global poverty. They refine and reaffirm the IDGs profiled earlier by industrial country ministers, adding an eighth specific goal for development cooperation and partnership on trade, finance, debt and aid.

Global Goals from Global Society

The crucial political meaning of these two sets of goals i.e. the Millennium Declaration and the MDGs is that, while authorized by national leaders, they came from society not from governments alone. Thousands of civil society organizations, hundreds of private sector leaders and 191 governments participated in these conferences culminating in the Millennium Summit in the fall of 2000. These goals are what Andrew

Cooper in his book on the UN conferences, 'Tests of Global Governance' (2004), calls "bottom up multilateralism". These two sets of goals are neither "UN Goals" nor official governmental goals only. While endorsed by governments at head of state/government level, they are indeed global goals from as well as for global society. In a very real sense, they came from society rather than being foisted on society. Therefore, they have process legitimacy derived from an inclusive consultative process across a range of inter-related issues.

Furthermore, they represent broad human aspirations that almost everyone can identify with. No one, rich or poor, wants to live in a world in which half the world is poor; no one wants to live in a world in which 2.4 billion people have no sanitation, or in a world in which children and mothers die needlessly because of lack of access to health care, or in a world in which forests-soils-water-fish-air and climate are threatened by human activity which can be managed more effectively. In terms of legitimacy derived from the values-aspirations-consensus-goal sequence, the Millennium Declaration and Millennium Development Goals represent the embodiment of broad aspirational legitimacy, not only because of the bottom up universal processes by which they were generated because of the content of the goal frameworks themselves.

While these frameworks can be seen as global goals for global society, the societal input from both NGOs and private sector groups largely was channeled through national delegations to these conferences and presented in the formal settings by national government officials. As Cooper indicates, "states still remain the principal agents within the UN-centered process of communication and negotiation." Global civil society organizations and international institutions do not supersede nation-state based representation at the global level. Global society in the global age is still predominantly governed by private and public sector leaders from national societies not from transnational entities. In the case of the series of UN conferences leading up to the Millennium frameworks, the channeling of values, aspirations and goals through national leaders into these global forums helped endow them with political legitimacy because of the primacy of the nation-state as the foundation of democracy. (See Brooks 2005)

In summary, the Millennium agenda appears to have three sources of legitimacy: bottom-up process legitimacy enhancing inclusiveness, aspirational legitimacy reflecting shared values, and political legitimacy derived from nation-state channeling of agency.

The Challenge of Implementation

In September 2005 the UN General Assembly brought together heads of state for the first time since the Millennium General Assembly in 2000 to review progress under the Millennium Declaration and the MDGs. Already, first reports are that the challenge of implementation is not surprisingly both difficult and urgent. Most observers think that the pace of action is not adequate to change the trend lines of the challenges. This implementation gap potentially adds still another dimension to the inadequacy mismatch of the international system to improve the global human condition.

As good as they are, these are reports by expert's not strategic guidance forged by political leaders. They are technical reports lacking political valence. They are better at seeing the needs by goal and by sector than they are at highlighting the inter-sectoral synergies and multi-sectoral dimensions. They make an excellent basis for shorter, more focused global action plans generated and endorsed by national political leaders to provide strategic guidance to key institutions and actors and to energize political momentum for mobilizing the policies, resources and actions necessary for achieving the MDGs by 2015.

The challenge of implementation of the Millennium Declaration and the MDGs are simply one more illustration of the need for global governance reform for the 21st century. Taking into account the foregoing categories, tensions and trade-offs, summit reform seems to be the most promising avenue for making a political breakthrough that can have multiplier effects throughout the international system and across a variety of domains. This is not to minimize the crucial importance of UN Security Council reform, or changing the voting shares in the BWIs or any number of other worthwhile efforts to strengthen the international system. Rather the opposite; it seems as if summit reform could complement these other reform efforts and in fact facilitate them rather than substitute for them.

Summit Reform

The G-7 summits were founded in 1978 primarily as a forum for coordination of economic policies among North America, Europe and Japan, the principal economies at the time. G-7 (Canada, France, Germany, Italy, Japan, the UK and the US) finance ministers still meet twice a year to monitor global economic conditions and to prepare the economic aspects of the G-7 heads of state summit agendas. Russia was added in the early 1990s to the summits but not to the ministers of finance. Otherwise, no institutional broadening of the G-7/8 mechanism has occurred in 27 years. Although heads of state from non-G-7/8 countries have increasingly been invited on an ad hoc basis for parts of the summits (lunches or dinners, for example) or for side events, they are not members of the summit mechanism. There is a thick and intensive network of finance, foreign affairs and even development cooperation officials of G-7 countries who work continuously to prepare and follow-up summit actions.

It is not hard to conclude that the summit mechanism is one aspect of the international system that is in need of reform. What is less well appreciated is how summit reform might become a major vehicle for addressing the broader issue of the mismatch between global problems and global institutions and processes as well as a device for generating reform momentum which could spill over into the UN, the BWIs and other spaces in the international community in need of reform. Summit reform, properly undertaken, could be the catalyst for systemic reform and for mobilizing resources for goal fulfillment.

Addressing Reluctance for Reform

On reflection, it is clear that one of the constraints on moving summit reform forward is an understandable reluctance on the part of current powers to dilute their control of the agenda and decision-making capacity (agency). It is equally clear that those new powers who might become institutional members of the summit group would be reluctant to go into what is now the G-7/8 group as minority members who could be swept along by the current powers on both the agenda and the conclusions. Some safeguards would be needed to provide assurances to both sets of countries to facilitate agreement. Secondly, there is also an understandable reluctance to move forward on expansion of the membership of the summit mechanism based on size alone, as in the proposal by Canadian Prime Minister Paul Martin to move the G-20 finance ministers group to head of state level summits which the Canadians now call the L-20. This proposal is not without appeal due to the fact that the G-20 finance ministers already have a satisfactory track record in their annual meetings since 1999. The non-G-8 countries in the G-20 are all large emerging market economies which are compelling because of the size of both their economies and their societies. (They are Argentina, Brazil, Mexico, China, India, Indonesia, Korea, Saudi Arabia, South Africa and Turkey.)

Together with the G-8 plus Australia, the G-20 comprises 64 per cent of the world's population as compared to 14 percent for the G-8. Expedient realism suggests a once-and-for-all leap from G-8 to L-20 to save the problem of opening the Pandora's box of the ideal membership. But there is sufficient reluctance to shutting out smaller, poorer developing countries and to under-representing Africa and the Middle East to forestall the L-20 proposal at the moment. Therefore, some modification of the L-20 idea may be necessary.

Safeguards against Pre-emption

Immediate safeguards from being taken hostage would be to establish decision-making procedures which protected each of the twelve core member countries. The general working method would be to resolve differences by compromise and try to achieve unanimous consensus among the L-12 on the agenda, on priorities and on policy decisions or recommendations. For example, where consensus cannot be reached because some core member's vital interests are at stake, a procedure for tabling an issue, which could then be brought back later if and when the core members' objections are dealt with. And a procedure for removing entirely an issue or decision from consideration might be put in place. A suggestion would be that any two core countries could table an issue, removing it for the time being from the discussion, with the understanding that it is not off the agenda entirely and could be brought back at a later time, providing the two core members concerns have been either met or taken care of by events. Another suggestion is that any four core members could in effect defeat an item or proposed decision by objection. This would remove the matter entirely from summit consideration for the foreseeable future, so as not to continuously clog up the agenda or provoke acrimony and conflict. The idea of these proposed procedures is to provide safeguards for both current and prospective members but not allow single country vetoes, as in the UN Security Council. Every singular objection requires at least one like-minded partner.

Evolutionary Representativeness

The ability of regimes to take in diverse opinions and to adjust to changed circumstances is an important feature to continuously upgrade capacity to deal with evolving contexts. (Epistemic reliability, in Robert Keohane's terminology. Keohane 2005, page 22.) There are two additional ways that might enhance representativeness legitimacy. There is increasing talk among Europeans that it would be acceptable in some specific institutional settings to reduce European representation to a single seat for the European Union. One such setting might be the IMF Board of Executive Directors; another could be the head of state summits. If the EU took one seat in the summits, it would reduce the core member group of the L-12 to nine countries, five industrial country seats and four developing country seats. This smaller sized group would enhance performance legitimacy by removing three extra seats while not stripping any single country or region of representation.

Also, an EU single chair might be an opportune moment to further enhance representativeness legitimacy by inviting an Islamic nation such as Egypt to take a core member seat at the table. It seems absolutely vital to include an Islamic nation and a Middle East country in the summit mechanism. Perhaps it can be done immediately. But if not, it might be better to go with what is feasible first i.e. add China, India, Brazil and South Africa which are less controversial and then move later to include an Islamic Middle Eastern country. If, for example, Egypt was added at the same moment that the EU took a single chair, the core group would be an L-10, with five industrial countries and five developing countries. The voting rules outlined above would still provide safeguards for all. The G-20 is an illustration of an effective group in which ten developing countries actually outnumber the nine industrial country members (when a G-7 member is president of the EU, which is the twentieth chair when the EU president is not a G-7 member country).

Another version of evolutionary representativeness was suggested orally by Kemal Dervis. It is to revisit the representativeness issue at some predetermined date in the future. For example, it could be agreed now, when a new summit grouping is formed, that in, say 2020, the membership/representativeness issue would be revisited and reviewed to see what current thinking and political perceptions are at the time. The most obvious seats that might come under review would be the developing country regional seats in Africa, the Middle East and Latin America. Since there is only one seat per region, it might be the case, according to the Dervis formulation, that any one of these regions might wish to claim a regional chair and elect a representative of the region for a period of, say, five years, to be reviewed and re-elected every five years. This could open up the issue of regional representation, which might be complex and contentious right now, even holding back the whole project of summit reform, but enhance the current reform proposal by not making once-and-forever decisions about representation and specifying a date certain in the future when the issue would be revisited.

Toward More Concerted Action on the Global Agenda

To summarize, there are several key drivers that compel action on summit reform. First, there is a vacuum at the apex of the international system for the implementation of the new global agenda, including the Millennium Declaration and the Millennium Development Goals, among other issues. UN ECOSOC is moribund; the World Bank-IMF ministerial committees (the IMFC and the Development Committee) are strictly speaking confined to the BWI agendas; the G-7/8 is too narrow in its country composition; there is now no mechanism for providing strategic guidance to the international system as a whole from the apex.

Second, there is an immense shift from the 20th century focus on specialization to the 21st century focus on inter-linkages among global challenges and on inter-sectoral synergies to be realized by dealing with them in an integrated rather than isolated fashion. This shift in the substantive foundations of the challenges humanity faces is mirrored by a configuration of international institutions, many of which are actually known as "specialized agencies", which are organized on 20th century principles. A major way to adjust the mismatch of the configuration of international institutions to the constellation of global challenges is for national political leaders to generate strategic guidance on the new inter-institutional relations which are required to adequately address the challenges and realize the inter-sectoral synergies embedded in the multi-sectoral MD and MDG agendas. Furthermore, only heads of state have the authority to address multi-sectoral programs involving multi-ministerial agendas within their countries as the necessary counterpart to inter-sectoral agenda for international institutions.

Third, the new global agenda potentially provides a new politics for democratic accountability through the relationship of global goals with quantifiable targets and indicators to monitoring and evaluation systems providing transparency and accountability. There is a new emphasis on results rather than efforts, outcomes rather than inputs which can create a new space for democratic politics and common endeavors. This new results orientation opens opportunities for political leadership to create new and more effective relations among different international institutions to generate greater synergies and higher yield outcomes in dealing with global issues. The injection of political leadership into these relationships can energize the linkages between different components of the international community, accelerating systemic reform. Linking leadership, vision, institutions and results can enhance accountability legitimacy of the international system.

Fourth, summit reform provides a potentially more flexible, feasible and facile avenue for transformational changes in global governance than other possible areas of reform. Creating new mandates and agendas for global governance and expanding the membership of the summit mechanism to include a combination of new core members and variable geometry for additional members depending on the issues and challenge up for discussion and decision is a way to combine enhanced representativeness and performance legitimacy in one move. Focusing on summit reform also capitalizes on the high political legitimacy associated with national government leaders in the international system. Summit reform seems to have the most solid foundation for apex leadership in the international system, the highest return in terms of effectiveness due to its small size, informal modality and un-bureaucratic nature, and the most diverse sources of representative legitimacy deriving from rotation, evolution, and expansion of the membership. By taking on humanity's goals for the 21st century, the summits will be seeking to reflect the aspirational legitimacy embodied in the goals themselves.

Politics provides the electricity that charges the international system with energy, resources and resolve to undertake major challenges. Translating national political leadership into global political leadership seems to be the best means of introducing new dynamics into the international system so that global governance processes can generate guidance, oversight and new relations of the international institutions necessary for the global challenges of the 21st century to be adequately addressed.

Roots in Environmental Justice

"Climate Justice is a vision to dissolve and alleviate the unequal burdens created by climate change. As a form of environmental justice, climate justice is the fair treatment of all people and freedom from discrimination with the creation of policies and projects that address climate change and the systems that create climate change and perpetuate discrimination."

Climate Justice as Evaluative Model

Climate Justice is a struggle over land, forest, water, culture, food sovereignty, collective and social rights; it is a struggle that considers justice at the basis of any solution; a struggle that supports climate solutions found in the practices and knowledge of those already fighting to protect and defend their livelihoods and the environment; a struggle that insists on a genuine systematic transformation in order to tackle the real causes of climate change. Climate Justice addresses four key themes: root causes, rights, reparations and participatory democracy.

Climate justice is a human-centered approach linking human rights and development. It protects the rights of the most vulnerable and aims at sharing the burdens and benefits of climate change and its resolution equitably and fairly'. It is about ensuring, both collectively and individually, that we have the ability to prepare for, respond to and recover from the impacts of climate change and the policies to mitigate or adapt to them by taking account of existing and projected vulnerabilities, resources and capabilities".

Justice can be used to validate completely opposing strategies, sometimes to simply defend vested interests or rights. Therefore the challenge for an ethical debate is to relate justice not only to single aspects but to view it from an overall, comprehensive perspective. The concept of justice should be universal, so that it is comprehensible and generally acceptable to all parties, regardless of whether they live in industrial or developing countries.

The interconnectedness and interdependence among all human rights, the principles of non-discrimination and equality, of democratic accountability, rule of law and political inclusiveness of all stakeholders in policy making, on climate change issues, remain basic and uncontroversial standards. Putting these and other related principles into practice, however, poses concrete challenges in terms of actual implementation. As an example, laws regulating water flow to ensure more efficient irrigation because of desertification or shift in rainfall patterns, is bound to advantage some local communities over others and, in some cases, it could even destroy livelihoods or cause trans-boundary harm to communities downstream.

The principles of indivisibility, interdependence and interrelatedness of human rights remind policy makers that civil and political rights, such as freedom of movement, the right to vote, free speech or freedom of association cannot be accorded priority over the rights to food, clean water, health and other economic, social and cultural rights, or the other way around. Practically speaking, the principles of the rule of law, genuine participation, inclusion and access to information, require that law and policy processes, as well as adjudication of disputes, be done according to the law and legal principles rather than by executive decree or in any other arbitrary manner. In this context, all affected communities, particularly vulnerable groups, must be genuinely, thoroughly and diligently consulted on the decisions which are likely to affect them with regard to climate-related issues. It requires that those who are unavoidably disadvantaged from climate policy decisions be adequately compensated for their loss, that the disadvantage itself is minimized and that; more generally, everyone has recourse to challenge law and policy in climate related matters so that injustices can be fairly redressed.

Debates over scaling powers within multilevel governance have become widely discussed in several related academic sub-disciplines, including economic federalism, political geography, EU studies, and international public policy. For example, conflicts over the appropriate scale or institutional level of policymaking characterize multilevel governance.

Under certain circumstances, experience gained and solutions found at one level of a particular scale might be appropriate to solve a problem at either a higher or a lower level of that scale. Thus scaling is a concern when searching for solutions to multi-scale and multilevel systems such as linked social-ecological systems. On the other hand, caution in transferring institutional arrangements is critical because an arrangement that fits one setting of a problem might not be suitable on another level or scale.

All parties, such as donor communities, governments, civil society, and others, must be aware that developing context-specific arrangements for all these elements is critical. The arrangements should take into account the environment in which local governmental and nongovernmental stakeholders have to operate, focusing on effective cooperation between them, the required capacity building and training of staff, joint information production and exchange, how to deal with corruption, and how to provide a positive incentive structure that stimulates accountability and responsiveness. The design principles have several potential uses in practice. First, by taking into account the issues they highlight, making and evaluating steps at different levels of governance can be made more adaptive. In this type of application, the design principles can be seen as diagnostic tools rather than blueprints for institutional reform. The specific solutions are almost always highly context dependent.

Second, the principles should be useful for exploring new and refining existing adaptation strategies by focusing more attention on their governance in particular, how decisions about particular strategies are reached. This can help overcome the frequent neglect of power relations and interests in the making of adaptation policy. Third, the principles may be useful not only to planning agencies and government processes but also to community-based organizations and the private sector actors interested in working with other stakeholders in proactive approaches to adaptation. Several of the roles implied by the design principles may be taken up effectively in some situations by non-state actors and multi-stakeholder bodies.

CHAPTER VI

THE TRADE REGIME COMPLEX AND MEGA REGIONAL'S: AN EXPLORATION FROM THE PERSPECTIVE OF INTERNATIONAL DOMINATION

Mega regional trade negotiations have become the subject of heated debate, above all in the context of the Transatlantic Trade and Investment Partnership (TTIP) and the Trans-Pacific Partnership (TPP). In the study, the argument is that the justice of the global order suffers from its institutional fragmentation into regime complexes. From a republican perspective, which aspires to non-domination as a guiding principles and idea of global justice, regime complexes raise specific and important challenges in that they open the door to specific forms of domination, thereby challenge a more optimistic outlook in regime complexes, which paints a positive normative picture of regime complexes, arguing that they enable the enhancement of democracy beyond the state and, consequently, have the potential to reduce the democratic deficit in global governance. By drawing attention to how regime complexes reinforce domination-related injustice, this study contributes an original perspective on mega-regionals and to exploring the implications of global justice as non-domination.

In the recent past, mega regional trade negotiations have become hotly debated and increasingly relevant, i.e. deep integration partnerships between countries or regions with a major share of world trade. One prominent example is the Transatlantic Trade and Investment Partnership (TTIP), which started being negotiated by the European Union (EU) and the United States (US) in 2013 in an environment of already dense, complicated and overlapping existing multilateral, bilateral, plurilateral and regional agreements. TTIP as well as the mega regional Trans-Pacific Partnership (TPP), which has been recently concluded by the US and eleven other countries along the Pacific Rim, and the China-lead Regional Comprehensive Economic Partnership (RCEP) in Asia, represent a trend towards an increasingly strong regionalization of trade governance via comprehensive free trade agreements and a progressive market opening outside the confines of the multilateral World Trade Organisation (WTO).

While the future of TTIP and TPP are not certain today, having been put on hold by the new US administration under President Trump, still the critique of the practices associated with megaregionals are relevant beyond these treaties themselves. The normative critique of TTIP and TPP is thus valuable even if these particular agreements were never implemented. At the same time, it is likely that the negotiations will be picked up again in one way or another in the near future, with European leaders and some high-level members of the US administration speaking out in favor of a TTIP-restart and the so-called 'TPP 11' grouping, all TPP-members but the US, being determined to forward the agreement. Moreover, many of the arguments made are relevant beyond the case of trade, for example in the context of other club governance arrangements like the G7 and the G20.

In which ways do the TTIP negotiations differ from the negotiations for other free trade agreements. TTIP aims to be deeper and larger than any other bilateral or regional trade agreement. Its depth, going far beyond many multilateral trade rules, the TTIP negotiations raise both trade and non-trade policy concerns, such as health and environmental protection. Moreover, due to its sheer size, representing around 30% of global trade and 60% of global GDP, TTIP has substantial effects on third countries and systemic effects for the system at large. In light of this, while TTIP has become the subject of heated debate, this debate often proceeds with an excessively narrow focus: The debate is primarily concerned with the impact of TTIP on Europe and the US and too little attention is being paid to the implications of this mega regional for the rest of the world and for the injustice of the global order. This study seeks to address the later question in the context of viewing TTIP as part of a so-called regime complex.

TTIP, if successful, would add another component to the existing sets of bilateral and regional as well as plurilateral and multilateral agreements with partly overlapping mandate and membership, otherwise known as the 'trade and investment regime complex'. While regime complexes have been studied empirically and this body of research continues to grow, so far, there have been only few detailed assessments of such complexes from a normative perspective. The question of how increasing institutional density and overlaps of international institutions should be assessed from a normative perspective has been significantly less in the scholarly limelight to date. More generally, research in international political theory has displayed a tendency to refrain from accounting for the fact that international institutions frequently display functional overlaps and that they often do not operate independently from each other.

Against this background, this study focuses on TTIP and other megaregionals and how they affect the trade regime complex and its normative assessment. By putting the spotlight on regime complexes from a normative perspective, the aim is to broaden research on the proliferation and growth of regime complexes. The institutionally fragmented international system puts in place a structure that enables international domination. From a republican perspective which aspires to non-domination as guiding principles and idea of global justice, regime complexes thus raise specific and important challenges in that they open the door to specific forms of domination. By drawing attention to how they reinforce domination-related injustice, this study contributes an original perspective on megaregionals and to exploring the implications of global justice as non-domination.

To be more precise the focus on mega the key characteristics of regime complexes contributes to highlighting the following inter-related points: Firstly, the existence of regime complexes can generate fragmentation that is sub-optimal from a republican perspective due to institutional opacities and challenges for power checks this gives rise to. Secondly, while there might be cases in which overlapping institutions lead to a better balancing of policy objectives in regime complexes, regime complexes also enable problematic cross-institutional strategies that undermine any kind of balancing processes from the start, above all 'forum shopping,' i.e. the strategic selection of an international decision-making venue, or 'regime shifting,' i.e. redefining the larger political context so as to ultimately reshape the system of rules itself in favor of those with power. Thirdly, the notion of regime complexes illustrates that the injustice of the global order depends also on the extent to which so-called 'institutional externalities', i.e. the effects overlapping international institutions create beyond their own institutional confines, amount to international domination.

Mapping the Trade Regime Complex

The 'trade and investment regime complex' (or, short, trade regime complex) is one among many other regime complexes, including the climate regime complex or the biodiversity or health regime complex.

'Regime complexes' are governance arrangements that do not consist of one single institution but of a set of inter and transnational institutions that display overlaps in their members and / or functions but are not coordinated by an overarching institution. Existing scholarship indicates that regime complexes have advantages and drawbacks. On the one hand, a complex comprising a plurality of institutions is often said to provide significant opportunities. It enables trial and error and could favour incremental adaptation to a changing environment. On the other hand, regime complexes are said to also come with drawbacks, such as redundancies and duplication, some confusion and the need for constant management of institutional interactions. Moreover, the institutional fragmentation of the international system may reduce international institutions' ability to create global public goods. In case of TTIP, these weaknesses could be considered as 'a fair price to pay to have a governance structure that is flexible, adaptive, creative and less vulnerable to crises. Yet, so far, it remains an open question whether this is a convincing perspective in the context of the trade regime complex. The trade regime complex has rapidly changed over the past years. An enormous increase of actors interested in and of institutions governing trade-related issues, inter and transnational has resulted in complex governance architecture. What has emerged is a densely populated regime complex for international trade that features pronounced overlaps among inter and transnational institutions and which are currently expanding in three dimensions:

Firstly, the trade regime complex is expanding in terms of institutions. Until the 2000s, the basic components of the complex were primarily intergovernmental organizations, regional customs unions and bilateral agreements. Recently, other institutional forms have mushroomed, including plurilateral sectoral agreements (e.g. the Anti-Counterfeiting Trade Agreement), venues for regulatory agencies (e.g. the International Competition Network), collaborations among intergovernmental organizations (e.g. the Standards and Trade Development Facility), private organizations (e.g. the International Accounting Standards Board) and, at the center of this article, megaregionals (e.g. TTIP and TPP). Secondly, the trade and investment complex is expanding in terms of issue areas. As known, rather than simply building on the WTO legacy with 'WTO-plus' commitments, it covers an increasing number of 'WTO-extra' issues such as anti-corruption, and tax evasion. These issues were not initially on the WTO agenda, but are now addressed by various trade initiatives and broadening the thematic frontiers of the trade and investment complex. Thirdly, the regime complex is expanding geographically. While, until recently, only a handful of countries were promoting trade and investment agreements, today, many countries are negotiating simultaneously on several in parallel, which underlines the high density and intricacy of the trade and investment regime complex. The trade complex is thus a system that can be analyzed as a whole.

International Domination and Global Justice

The republican concept of freedom of non-domination can be understood as the absence of the power to interfere arbitrarily with agents' choices is they individuals or corporate agents. Domination is the subjection to the arbitrary power of another actor. Power, in turn, can be said to be arbitrary when it is not subjected to appropriate checks and controls.

While there is a growing literature on non-domination in the global arena, regime complexes have not yet been addressed from that perspective. The large majority of the literature on non-domination in the global arena does not question the individualistic perspective that characterizes the domestic (neo) republican point of view. However, going beyond the focus on individuals, an emerging literature is increasingly exploring the domination of states as well. Building on this literature, this study puts the spotlight on international domination and the domination of states.

For instance, in his recent work, Philip Pettit has put forward an international ideal of non-domination, in which he moves beyond the two-dimensional picture that focuses on the realization of individual freedom as non-domination through a non-dominating state by including a third dimension that takes into account the potential of states themselves being dominated. As Pettit puts it: 'In a slogan, the state ought to be an internationally undominated, domestically undominating defender of its citizens' freedom as non-domination.'

In a recent study, Cecile Laborde and Miriam Ronzoni also put the spotlight on the domination of states, arguing that globalization generates new opportunities for domination and that this domination amounts to global injustice. For example, citizens in dominated states are themselves exposed to domination since a state that does not enjoy basic non-domination loses 'internal problem-solving capacity' with respect to political issues that directly concern it: 'This occurs when states are directly enmeshed in colonial, imperial or post-colonial relations, but also when their integration into the global order operates on terms that are ostensibly non-coercive, yet exhibit features of power imbalance, dependency and arbitrariness.' In addition to other features of globalization and the global order, TTIP, raises serious worries in this respect.

Going forward, one should bear in mind the following distinction between two forms of domination: increases of domination as a result of actions by other states ('dominium') and domination as a result of the exercise of international governance institutions ('imperium'). In what follows, while with an argument that can be relevant both in the case of 'dominium' and in the case of 'imperium', the latter type of domination, puts the spotlight on domination in the former sense, i.e. on domination between states.

International Domination in the Trade Regime Complex

It is crucial to clarify the normative baseline for arguing that regime complexes and institutional fragmentation contribute to international domination. In a world without TTIP and similar mega regional, trade issues would be regulated mainly within the multilateral WTO. Due to huge economic power imbalances between states and the informal use of arbitrary power by states in trade negotiations, even the seemingly representative WTO, can be said to be characterized by intra-institutional domination. There would be no international domination related to trade negotiations in the absence of megaregionals. It is rather that TTIP and similar agreements worsen the situation with respect to international domination in comparison to a world without TTIP and other megaregionals. Another domination-related concern, is the type of domination that might subordinate citizens of one state directly under the power of some other state, the power of some supranational governance institution, or the power of some foreign private actor e.g. corporations etc.

Secondly, opportunities for forum shopping and regime shifting and, thirdly, their repercussion on negotiations in the multilateral forum of the WTO.

Megaregionals and International Domination

Putting the emphasis on domination between states by focusing on:

(1) How states are directly impacted by regime complexes that entail megaregionals. In the context of assessing the more direct impact of megaregionals, the ability of different types of actors to make use of the changing nature of the trade regime complex and the implications of global rule-making via megaregional trade agreements need to be taken

into account.

(2) How do megaregionals increase international domination between states. Do mega regional trade negotiations not rather provide room for more balanced justifications in the trade regime complex? According to Kuyper, regime complexes enable cross-institutional strategies like 'forum-shopping' and 'regime-shifting', which in turn, according to him, enables weaker actors to contest existing institutionalized inequalities and enhance the realization of core democratic values, such as equal participation.

(3) Yet, the ability to make use of such strategies strongly differs across actors. Less powerful states usually lack the ability to resort to strategies like forum shopping and regime shifting in the context of the trade regime complex while powerful states can opportunistically use these strategic approaches to create settings and or rules in their favor. The disadvantage of poorer and weaker states in the global order is thereby reinforced because they cannot adequately take advantage of or exercise new opportunities that megaregionals offer. In comparison to states who lack power, powerful countries have much less to lose if they shift away from the WTO as a forum for multilateral negotiations and are turning towards a new type of 'megaregional forum': Because of their power, they are much less dependent on the WTO to negotiate the trade rules of the future since they can shape trade negotiations outside the WTO in their favor. In fact, the availability of cross-institutional strategies in an institutionally fragmented global order characterized by the existence of manifold regime complexes is, at least in part, 'the result of a calculated strategy by powerful states to create a legal order that both closely reflects their interests and only they have the capacity to alter'.

Less powerful countries, in contrast, depend more on the multilateral forum of the WTO than those with power. They need the multilateral forum of the WTO in order to build coalitions to be able to defend their needs and interests and in many cases to have a voice in the first place. The WTO is the negotiation framework in which developing countries can assert their interests more effectively than during the megaregional negotiations, where they often lack the upper hand if they are involved at all and not excluded from the start like in the case of TTIP. In the WTO, especially during the more recent sets of negotiations, less powerful countries have typically joined forces and successfully built coalitions in order to oppose trade rules that were not in their interest or negotiate in favor of trade rules they preferred and that corresponded to their national development levels. However, negotiations in sub-groups beyond the multilateral system e.g. in the context of megaregional negotiations limit this kind of coalition-building, which allows advanced economies to play competing trade partners off against one another.

In sum, poorer and weaker states cannot adequately take advantage or exercise the new opportunities that regime complexes offer, thereby worsening their relative position, which amounts to a restriction of their freedom as non-domination. The availability of cross-institutional strategies in an institutionally fragmented global order thus enables domination by powerful actors. Regime complexes contribute to structurally undermining the freedom of states in problematic ways and contribute to injustice by increasing the potential for, or the existence of, domination.

The above also underlines that less powerful countries are directly affected by being exposed to stronger domination in the context of megaregional negotiations rather than in multilateral negotiations in the WTO due to their more direct exposure to power inequalities in light of much fewer (e.g. in the case of TPP) or no options (e.g. in the case of TTIP) for coalition-building. To illustrate, consider the example of the case of Vietnam in the context of the TPP negotiations. For instance, TPP offered the US 'a bargaining chip to demand compliance with labour standards,' which the US used to ask Vietnam to sign a bilaterally negotiated 'Labour Action Plan'. Whereas improving workers' rights is an important objective from a normative perspective, developing countries often view it as a challenge that might decrease their competitive advantage and therefore hesitate to take on binding commitments in that regard.

More generally, TPP confronts developing countries with many issues with ambivalent development impacts that, so far, do not figure prominently at the multilateral level, including commitments on investment or stricter rules on intellectual property rights. For example, protection for investors mainly caters to the interests of industrialized countries, with 85 percent of all related investor-state complaints originating from there and with developing countries frequently being disadvantaged by the burdens of a strict investment protection regime. While developing countries and many emerging economies have successfully opposed including these issues in multilateral trade negotiations due to effective coalition-building in light of their questionable development impacts (Hopewell 2015), they are now re-entering through the back door in the context of multi-regionals. For example, TPP includes rules that strengthen intellectual property rights, which could make it harder to access affordable medication. Restriction on freedom of states in the international context is not necessarily bad; for example, environmental protection regulations may limit the freedom of states but would not necessarily constitute an injustice. However, in the case under consideration, the restrictions at stake are indeed problematic because they amount to arbitrary interference while limiting many states' freedom to have a say in shaping the trade rules of the future.

Trade-rule-making on the basis of mega regional trade agreements entails more inequality than multilateral trade-rule-making because less powerful countries have fewer if any opportunities to create coalitions to veto the proposals of the more powerful or shape trade-rules in line with their needs and interests. Moreover, mega regional negotiations are much less formalized than multilateral ones. Informal institutions, which are characterized by rules that are vague or non-binding, typically favor the powerful over the weaker actors because they enable them to take advantage of the flexibility of informality to their own benefit. In sum, the dominating nature of the megaregional approach to rule-setting thus becomes apparent once we compare it to the situation without megaregionals when other states used to have more input into the making of global trade-rules.

In addition, megaregionals give rise to concerns because they preclude numerous countries from the negotiations that determine future global trade rules. Megaregionals are attempts by the old powers, above all the US and the EU, to set new rules of play for the world economy. These trade rules then become the new 'standard' trade rules and are being 'diffused' globally by the EU and the US when they use them as blueprints once they start negotiating with other countries. Third parties, i.e. all the countries excluded from megaregional negotiations, are likely to have to agree to them in future negotiations with the EU and the US; these third parties thus end up being rule-takers with regard to many of the important trade rules of the future.

The setting of global rules and standards by powerful actors continues the wrongful playing of sides as the old powers shape future global trade rules in line with their interests. Many of these trade rules negotiated in the context of megaregionals, as indicated above, are in conflict with developing countries' needs and interests, with dubious effects on their economy and potentially on their internal problem-solving capacities, in turn undermining domestic justice. Megaregionals thus also raise concerns from a global justice perspective because they have important implications due to their ambition to create global rules that are likely to go against the interest of less powerful developing countries.

In the context of megaregionals, developing countries fear being left behind, especially in relation to their export competitors, and are exposed to power inequalities even if they are not involved in any negotiations with powerful countries; they are thus increasingly under pressure, due to the huge market power of megaregionals, to adopt the kind of trade rules and standards the megaregional negotiating partners have taken on even if they are not negotiating with the major megaregional powers. The arbitrary interference megaregional negotiations give rise to, arguably amounting to a case of international domination can thus be pertinent even if there is no direct interference. To illustrate: Some of the developing countries affected by Vietnam's improved market access to the US due to the Vietnamese economy being part of the TPP negotiations, e.g. Pakistan or Bangladesh, are considering to join TPP in the future to protect their export competitive industries, despite not really being ready to adopt many of the agreement's provisions on the controversial issues just mentioned and despite having had no opportunity to help shape the megaregional. This shows that, in addition to domination by states in more or less direct ways, domination can also occur while direct interference is absent. Even, third countries that are not part of negotiations for TTIP, TPP or similar approaches, will never be directly or indirectly pressured into taking over rules and standards, megaregionals will generate negative economic consequences for them. One reason for negative effects of megaregionals on third countries is that such trade agreements in contrast to multilateral ones lead to trade diversion effects for excluded parties, as already argued in Jacob Viner's seminal work. For example, in the case of TTIP, EU goods would become relatively cheaper for US consumers and 'the US will substitute away from third countries' goods towards EU goods.' Poor developing countries excluded from megaregionals are therefore likely to suffer losses in trade and competitiveness, Countries that are relatively insignificant in terms of their status as economic and geopolitical partners have the most to fear from megaregionals, as they have no involvement whatsoever in drafting the rules of the future; emerging economies, on the other hand, are in a better position to enter the competition for regional trade partnerships as a result of their economic and political weight and shape their future, as demonstrated by China's involvement in the RCEP negotiations with 15 other Asian countries. In contrast to this, African countries have yet to participate in negotiations regarding a mega regional agreement and risk becoming even more marginalized in the future.

When 'poor countries ingratiate themselves to please the richer states they depend upon, without the stronger states making any explicit demand or threat, we have a paradigmatic case of international domination without interference' (Laborde and Ronzoni (2016), p. 289).

Since megaregionals redirect trade flows, these countries also have a harder time accessing capital and technology. Simulations of the implications of TTIP indicate that a number of developing countries should expect to suffer losses. Being subjected to this form of arbitrary interference, and hence domination, can affect the internal problem-solving capacities of these states, which in turn undermines domestic justice.

The other type of domination, which occurs as a result of the exercise of international governance institutions ('imperium'), is relevant, for example, when states only face one large and powerful international governance institution, from which there is no escaping. It has been argued that this is the case, for example, in the context of the WTO. At first sight, one might therefore argue that, at least in this respect, the rise of megaregionals, offering alternatives to and potentially limiting domination by the WTO, and the trend towards the fragmentation of the trade regime is domination-reducing rather than the opposite. Yet, as argued in the next section, the creation of alternatives in the WTO is likely to even increase domination in the context of the WTO.

Megaregionals and Repercussions on the Multilateral System

The extent to which institutions open the door for international domination can also depend on the effects these institutions create on other international institutions and their governance domains. In other words, there is a need to analyze 'institutional externalities' when we assess the justice of the global order, i.e. the effects international institutions create beyond their own institutional confines, including on other (democratic) international institutions: that an assessment of international domination needs to be sensitive to the effects international institutions create in domains that lie beyond their own.

In the case of megaregionals, one pertinent question is how they affect the multilateral trading system. It is argued that megaregional negotiations have important repercussions by strongly intensifying the exposure of less powerful states to power inequalities within multilateral negotiations. The reason is that TTIP and TPP increase the pressure, especially on less powerful states, to make compromises in the WTO for fear the US and the EU will lose all interest in the multilateral forum. The US has made clear that without a new agenda in line with US interests in the WTO, this is what is likely to happen. Indeed, against the background of the proliferation of megaregional agreements, at the 2015 WTO Ministerial, many member states were under immense pressure to agree to the proposed Nairobi outcome because the lack of any outcome could have contributed to undermining the WTO even more. In the words of a commentator, the lack of an outcome in Nairobi would have fostered 'the end of the consensus-based organization as a meaningful negotiating forum and usher in an era dominated instead by megaregional deals like the Trans-Pacific Partnership, where the US gets to choose who's in and who's out'. According to other observers, if developing countries are 'not going to play ball in the WTO, the US and EU will pick up the ball and go play somewhere else.' From normative perspective, this would be highly regrettable. Especially less powerful, poorer countries need the WTO to get their voices heard. If, like in the case of the WTO, the outside options are better for the dominant member states than for the subordinate ones, deadlocks within existing institutions can lead to stronger domination within and by existing institutions and to the creation of new institutions, for example in the context of regime shifts, which do not only tend to reproduce but may even deepen inequalities compared to the status quo ante of the original institution at stake.

Concluding Observations

The analysis of megaregionals as part of the trade regime complex from the perspective of international non-domination shows that the justice of the global order suffers from its institutional fragmentation because this structural feature enables strong states to dominate weaker ones. Regime complexes open the door for international domination and TTIP and other megaregionals offer an illustration of that process.

The argument is that regime complexes generate problematic institutional opacities and enable cross-institutional strategies like forum shopping and regime shifting that opens the door for international domination and that the injustice of the global order depends also on the extent to which institutional externalities and inequalities amount to arbitrary interference and hence international domination. Moreover, it is argued that the mechanisms of forum shopping or regime shifting underline the importance of situating power relations in individual organizations, e.g.

the WTO, within a larger institutional context, i.e. the regime complex of trade. The shopping as well as shifting benefits some members of the pre-existing regime of the WTO, namely the dominant ones, more than others by allowing them to opt for a forum more likely to produce their preferred outcomes.

Regarding megaregionals, the argument is that TTIP shows that domination does not only occur through supra-national institutions or private actors or direct state domination but can also take place in more indirect ways: TTIP is a bilateral institution that is shaped by two powerful trade partners but that has implications for the system at large, which causes global repercussions, above all for those with less power, and raises concerns about international domination. Relatedly, TTIP illustrates that arbitrary power is not just abused within existing institutions but also to set-up new ones. As indicated above, this is relevant beyond the case of trade, e.g. in the context of the G7 and the G20. TTIP is hence not only an important and interesting case in order to reflect on regime complexes from a normative perspective but also to ponder the role of club governance. Club governance can be problematic if there are strong externalities, i.e. when exclusive clubs set rules that have global implications. TTIP is an example of a club that sets the club rules for its members but, at the same time, has global effects and sets rules that are likely to be a blueprint for other institutions in the future, to which states will be subject that have not had a say in TTIP and the set of trade rules it generates.

It is often being argued that the institutions that govern the global economy and their policies have been biased against developing countries and have contributed to persisting international inequalities as, for the most part; developing countries did not belong to the group of powerful actors in global governance. But as countries such as China, India and Brazil are becoming more and more important, the dominance of the old powers is said to have come increasingly under pressure. In light of these developments, it has been discussed whether the rising powers challenge the existing international economic order and whether they foster alternative and potentially more equitable approaches to governing the global economy. A closer look at more recent developments in the global trading system indicates that the traditional powers actually seem to retain their dominance in global trade governance with institutional inequalities being reproduced and even deepened within and beyond the WTO. The powerful increasingly abandon the WTO to pursue their interests outside of the multilateral system, at the cost of the weakest states in the international system. Megaregionals hence suggest that we might have to pay more attention to the dynamics between old and newly rising powers and how these dynamics affect the global order and the scope for domination.

What does this imply for fostering non-domination in the global realm? According to Laborde and Ronzoni, there is a need for stronger institutional regulation of global affairs to safeguard the basic non-domination of states and to achieve this objective; we need to pursue a multifaceted strategy, which includes power countering, distribution, democratization, constitutionalization and regulation. The first option, so-called 'power countering', suggests that until we realize the non-domination of states, we 'have reasons to support strategies of resistance on behalf of those states which are more likely to be at the worse end of international domination'. As they mention, power countering can lead to an impasse and this is what happened in the context of the WTO Doha negotiations where rising powers started to resist. Yet, as indicated above, this strategy was, at least in some ways, counter-productive: international domination was arguably not avoided but intensified, namely outside the WTO due to the regime shifting towards megaregionals, from which many rising powers are excluded. Megaregionals hence stress the difficulties of achieving the right kind of non-domination strategy. They show, for example, that the strategy of power countering can have unintended consequences and might backfire, especially for the weakest states in the international order.

Future research should focus on discussing and investigating the right kind of strategy to avoid international domination against the background of mushrooming regime complexes. For instance, the impact of TTIP on developing countries and on the global order depends on the manner in which the agreement is drafted and what kind of trade rules they contain. More generally, scholars might discuss and investigate, for instance, to what extent the increasing relevance of regime complexes might call for novel strategies to safeguard basic non-domination, say on the basis of some sort of rules that regulate the creation of new institutions that have global implications or on the basis of more extensive constitutionalization.

REFERENCES

Academic Foundation. Security Implications of Climate Change for India, report of the Institute for Defence Studies and Analyses Working Group. New Delhi: Academic Foundation, 2009.

Aggestam, Lisbeth. “Introduction: Ethical Power Europe.” International Affairs 84 (2008): 1- 11.

Alecu de Flers, Nicole. EU Foreign Policy and the Europeanization of Neutral States: Comparing Irish and Austrian foreign policy. Abingdon: Routledge, 2012.

Andreatta, Filippo. “The European Union’s International Relations: A Theoretical View.” In International Relations and the European Union, edited by Christopher Hill and Michael Smith, 21-43. Second edition. Oxford: Oxford University Press, 2011.

Acemoglu, Daron, Simon Johnson, and James Robinson. 2002. Reversal of fortune: Geography and institutions in the making of the modern world income distribution. *Q*uarterly Journal of Economics 117 (4): 1231–94.

Acemoglu, Daron, Simon Johnson, and James Robinson. 2001. The colonial origins of comparative development: An empirical investigation. American Economic Review 91 (5): 1369–1401.

Adsera, Alicia, and Carles Boix. 2002. Trade, democracy and the size of the public sector: The political under-pinnings of openness. International Organization 56 (2): 229–62.

Alesina, Alberto, and David Dollar. 2000. Who gives foreign aid to whom and why? Journal of Economic Growth 5(1): 33–63.

Aisbett, Emma. 2005. Why are the critics so convinced that globalization is bad for the poor? National Bureau of Economic Research Working Study 11066.

Andrew F. Cooper (2004), Tests of Global Governance: Canadian Diplomacy and United Nations World Conferences, Tokyo: United Nations University Press.

Bagwell, Kyle, and Robert W. Staiger. 2002. The economics of the world trading system. Cambridge: MIT Press.

Bailey, Michael A., Judith Goldstein, Barry R. Weingast. 1997. The institutional roots of American trade policy: Politics, coalitions, and international trade. World Politics 49(3): 309–338.

Barnett, Michael N., and Martha Finnemore. 1999. The politics, power, and pathologies of international organizations. International Organization 53 (4): 699–732.

Bhagwati, Jagdish. 2004. In defense of globalization. New York: Oxford University Press.

Bird, Graham, and Dane Rowlands. 2001. IMF Lending: How is it affected by economic, political and institutional factors? Policy Reform 4 (3): 243–70.

Blake, Michael. 2001. Distributive justice, state coercion and autonomy. Philosophy and Public Affairs 30 (3): 257–95.

Boughton, James M. 2001. Silent revolution: The International Monetary Fund 1979–1989. Washington, DC: IMF.

Buchanan, Allen. 2000. Rawls's law of peoples: Rules for a vanished Westphalian world. Ethics 110 (4): 697–721.

Bueno de Mesquita, Bruce, and Hilton Root, eds. 2002. Governing for prosperity. New Haven: Yale University Press.

Burnside, Craig, and David Dollar. 2000. Aid, policies and growth. American Economic Review 90(4): 847–68.

Barry, Brian M. 1995. Justice as impartiality. Oxford: Oxford University Press.

Beitz, Charles R. 1979. Political theory and international relations. Princeton: Princeton University Press.

Babcicky, Philipp. "A Conflict-Sensitive Approach to Climate Change Adaptation." Peace Review: A Journal of Social Justice 25, no. 4 (2013): 480–88.

Barnett, Jon, and W. Neil Adger. "Climate Change, Human Security and

Violent Conflict." Political Geography 26 (2007): 639–55.

Bernhagen, P., Bräuninger, T., 2005. Structural power and public policy: A signaling model of business lobbying in democratic capitalism. Polit. Stud. 53, 43–64.

Bodansky, Daniel. "Legitimacy in International Law and International Relations." In Interdisciplinary Perspectives on International Law and International Relations, edited by Jeffrey L. Dunoff and Mark A. Pollack, 321-342. Cambridge: Cambridge University Press, 2013.

Bradford, Anu, and Eric Posner. "Universal Exceptionalism in International Law." Harvard International Law Journal 52 (2011): 3-54.

Bretherton, Charlotte, and John Vogler. The European Union as a Global Actor. Second edition. London: Routledge, 2006.

Brunnée, Jutta, and Stephen J. Toope. "Constructivism and International Law." In Interdisciplinary Perspectives on International Law and International, edited by Jeffrey L. Dunoff and Mark A. Pollack, 125-142. Cambridge: Cambridge University Press, 2013.

Bontis, N., Fitz-Enz, J., 2002. Intellectual capital ROI: a causal map of human capital antecedents and consequents. J. Intellect. Cap. 3, 223–247.

Büchner, C.I.R., 2013. Social background, educational attainment and labor market integration: an exploration of underlying processes and dynamics. ROA, Maastricht University, Maastricht.

Borgerson, Scott G. "Arctic Meltdown."Foreign Affairs 87, no. 2 (2008): 63–77.

Brauch, Hans Günter, and Jürgen Scheffran. "Introduction: Climate Change, Human Security, and Violent Conflict in the Anthropocene." In Climate Change, Human Security and Violent Conflict, ed. Jürgen Scheffran, Michael Brzoska, Hans Günter Brauch, Peter Michael Link, and Janpeter Schilling. Heidelberg: Springer, 2012.

Breisinger, Clemens, Tingju Zhu, Perrihan Al Riffai, Gerald Nelson, Richard Robertson, Jose Funes, and Dorte Verner. "Global and Local Economic Impacts of Climate Change in Syria and Options for Adaptation." IFPRI Discussion Study no. 01091, International Food Policy Research Institute, Washington, DC, June 2011.

Brown, Oli, Anne Hammill, and Robert McLeman. "Climate Change as the 'New' Security Threat: Implications for Africa." International Affairs 83, no. 6 (2007): 1141–54.

Brzoska, Michael. "Climate Change as a Driver of Security Policy." In Climate Change, Human Security and Violent Conflict, ed. Jürgen Scheffran, Michael Brzoska, Hans Günter Brauch, Peter Michael Link, and Janpeter Schilling. Heidelberg: Springer, 2012.

Buhaug, Halvard, and Ole Magnus Theisen. "On Environmental Change and Armed Conflict." In Climate Change, Human Security and Violent Conflict, ed. Jürgen Scheffran, Michael Brzoska, Hans Günter Brauch, Peter Michael Link, and Janpeter Schilling. Heidelberg: Springer, 2012.

Byravan S, Rajan S. "Providing new homes for climate change exiles." Climate Policy. No. 6 (2006): 247–252.

Cavicchio, C., 2008. Council perspectives; Immigration and corporate philanthropy.

Claes, Monica, and Maartje de Visser. "Reflections on comparative method in European constitutional law." In Practice and Theory in Comparative Law, edited by Maurice Adams and Jacco Bomhoff, 143-169. Cambridge: Cambridge University Press, 2012.

Cooper, Robert. The Post-modern State and the World Order. London: Demos, 2000.

Court of Justice of the European Union. Case 294/83 Parti écologiste 'Les Verts' [1986] ECR 01339.

Case 4/79 Nold v Commission [1975] ECR 00491.

Case 222/84 Johnston [1986] ECR 01651.

Craig, Paul. "Constitutions, Constitutionalism, and the European Union." European Law Journal 7 (2001): 126-135.

Cremona, Marise, et al.. ASEAN's External Agreements: Law, practice and the question for collective action. Cambridge: Cambridge University Press, forthcoming 2015.

CEDEFOP, 2014. Valuing diversity: guidance for labor market integration of migrants (Cedefop working study No. No. 24). Publications Office of the European Union, Luxembourg.

CEDEFOP, 2011. Migrants, minorities, mismatch? Skill mismatch among migrants and ethnic minorities in Europe (CEDEFOP Research Studies No. 5516). Publications Office of the European Union, Luxembourg.

Caney, Simon. 2001. International Distributive Justice, Political Studies 49 (4): 974–97.

Chen, Shaohua, and Martin Ravaillon. 2005. How have the worlds poorest fared since the early 1980s? World Bank Staff Study 3341.

Constant, A.F., 2014. Do migrants take the jobs of native workers? IZA World Labor.

Climate Change 2014: Impacts, Adaptation, and Vulnerability. Working Group II, 5th Assessment Report. Cambridge: Cambridge University Press, 2014.

Colin I. Bradford, Jr. and Johannes F. Linn (2004), "Global Economic Governance at a Crossroads: Replacing the G-7 with the G-20", Washington: The Brookings Institution, Policy Brief No.131, April 2004.

Council of the European Union. "Council Conclusions on EU water diplomacy." Foreign Affairs Council meeting, Brussels, July 22, 2013.

Coppel, J., Dumont, J.-C., Visco, I., 2001. Trends in immigration and economic consequences (No. No. 284), OECD Economics Department Working Studies, OECD Publishing.

Crul, M., Doomernik, J., 2003. The Turkish and Moroccan second generation in the Netherlands: Divergent trends between and polarization within the two groups1. Int. Migr. Rev. 37, 1039–1064.

Cullity, Garrett. 1994. International aid and the scope of kindness. Ethics 105 (1): 99–127.

Donnelly, Jack. Realism and International Relations. Cambridge: Cambridge University Press, 2000.

Dunoff, Jeffrey L., and Mark A. Pollack. "International Law and International Relations: Introducing an Interdisciplinary Dialogue." In Interdisciplinary Perspectives on International Law and International

Relations, edited by Jeffrey L. Dunoff and Mark A. Pollack, 3-32. Cambridge: Cambridge University Press, 2013.

Delgado Casteleiro, Andrés and Joris Larik. "The Duty to Remain Silent: Limitless Loyalty in EU External Relations?" European Law Review 36

David Brooks (2005), "Loudly, With a Big Stick", New York Times, April 14, 2005.

DAC, Development Assistance Committee (1996), Shaping the 21st Century: The Contribution of Development Cooperation, Paris, OECD, and May 1996.

Defense Intelligence Agency. "Intelligence Community Assessment on Global Water Security." ICA 2012-08. Washington: US Department of State, February 2, 2012.

Delaney, David, and Helga Leitner. "The Political Construction of Scale." Political Geography 16, no. 2 (1997): 93–97.

Dadush, U., 2014. The effect of low-skilled labor migration on the host economy, KNOMAD Working Study 1. KNOMAD.

Dustmann, C., Frattini, T., 2014. The fiscal effects of immigration to the UK. Econ. J. 124, F593–F643.

Dustmann, C., Frattini, T., Preston, I.P., 2013. The effect of immigration along the distribution of wages. Rev. Econ. Stud. 80, 145–173.

Edward O. Wilson (1998), Consilience: The Unity of Knowledge, New York: Alfred A. Knopf. CIB: 17 May 2005

European Commission. (2014). Diversity Management implementation and impact amongst Diversity Charter signatories in the European Union. European Union.

Erian, Wadid, Bassem Katlan, and Ouldbdey Babah. "Drought vulnerability in the Arab region: Special case study: Syria." Damascus: Global Assessment Report on Disaster Risk Reduction, 2011.

Elster, Jon. 1978. Logic and society: Contradictions and possible worlds. New York: John Wiley.

Easterly, William, and Ross Levine. 2002. Tropics, germs and crops: How endowments influence economic development. National Bureau of Economic Research Working Study 9106.

Easterly, William. 2001a. The elusive quest for growth: Economists' adventures and misadventures in the tropics. Cambridge: MIT Press.

Fantu Cheru and Colin I. Bradford (2005), "The Planet at Risk: Mobilizing Resources for Global Human Security", in Helsinki Process Secretariat (2005), Helsinki Process Studies on Global Economic Agenda, Helsinki: Foreign Ministries Publications, pp. 9-61.

Frankenberg, Günter. "Comparative constitutional law." In The Cambridge Companion to Comparative Law, edited by Mauro Bussani and Ugo Mattei, 171-190. Cambridge: Cambridge University Press, 2012.

Franck, Thomas. Political Questions/Judicial Answers: Does the rule of law apply to foreign affairs? Princeton, NJ: Princeton University Press, 1992.

Finer, S.E., Vernon Bogdanor and Bernard Rudden. Comparing Constitutions. Oxford: Clarendon Press, 1995.

Forman, Fonna, and Gerry Mackie. "Introduction: New frontiers in global justice." Critical Review of International Social and Political Philosophy 16 (2013): 151-161.

Foged, M., Peri, G., 2016. Immigrants' Effect on Native Workers: New Analysis on Longitudinal Data. Am. Econ. J. Appl. Econ. 8, 1–34.

Geddes, Andrew, and William Somerville. "Migration and Environmental Change in International Governance: The Case of the European Union." Environment and Planning C: Government and Policy 30, no. 6 (2012): 1015–28.

Gilligan, Michael J. 1997. Empowering exporters. Ann Arbor, MI: University of Michigan Press.

Gould, Erica R. 2004. Money talks: The International Monetary Fund, conditionality and supplementary financiers. Unpublished manuscript.

Grant, Ruth W., and Robert O. Keohane. 2005. Accountability and abuses of power in world politics. American Political Science Review 99 (1): 29–43.

Gruber, Lloyd. 2000. Ruling the world: Power politics and the rise of supranational institutions. Princeton: Princeton University Press.

Gerhardt, Hans, Philip E. Steinberg, Jeremy Tasch, Sandra J. Fabiano, and Rob Shields. "Contested Sovereignty in a Changing Arctic." Annals of the Association of American Geographers 100, no. 4 (2010): 992–1002.

German Advisory Council on Global Change. "Climate Change as a Security Risk." Berlin: WBGU, 2008.

Green, K.A., López, M., Wysocki, A., Kepner, K., 2002. Diversity in the workplace: Benefits, challenges, and the required managerial tools. Univ. Fla. Coop. Ext. Serv. Inst. Food Agric. Science.

Greenstone, M., Looney, A., 2010. Ten economic facts about immigration. Hamilton Project, The Brookings Institution.

Global Commission on the Economy and Climate (Global Commission). Better Growth Better Climate: The New Climate Economy Report. Washington, DC: World Resources Institute, September 2014, p. 152.

Governing the Commons: The Evolution of Institutions for Collective Action. New York: Cambridge University Press, 1990.

Gowricharn, R., 2002. Integration and social cohesion: the case of the Netherlands. J. Ethn. Migr. Stud. 28, 259–273.

Gheciu, Alexandra. "Security Institutions as Agents for Socialization? NATO and Post-Cold War Central and Eastern Europe." International Organization 59 (2005): 973-1012.

Gilpin, Robert. "The Richness of the Tradition of Political Realism." In Neorealism and Its Critics, edited by Robert O. Keohane, 301-321. New York, NY: Columbia University Press, 1986.

Ginsburg, Tom, Svitlana Chernykh and Zachary Elkins. "Commitment and Diffusion: How and why national constitutions incorporate international law." University of Illinois Law Review (2008): 201-237.

Gnesotto, Nicole, and Giovanni Grevi, The New Global Puzzle: What World for the EU in 2025? Paris: EUISS, 2006.

Goldsmith, Jack and Daryl Levinson. "Law for States: International Law, Constitutional Law, Public Law." Harvard Law Review 122 (2009): 1791-

1868.

Haldén, Peter. The Geopolitics of Climate Change. Stockholm: Swedish Defence Research Agency, 2007.

Henkin, Louis. The Rights of Man Today. London: Stevens, 1979.

Hurd, Ian. "Constructivism." In The Oxford Handbook of International Relations, edited by Christian Reus-Smit and Duncal Snidal, 298-316. Oxford: Oxford University Press, 2010.

Hurrell, Andrew, and Terry Macdonald. "Ethics and Norms in International Relations." In Handbook of International Relations, edited by Walter Carlsnaes, Thomas Risse and Beth A. Simmons, 57-84. Second edition. London: SAGE, 2013.

Hyde-Price, Adrian. "A 'tragic actor'? A realist perspective on 'ethical power Europe." International Affairs 84 (2008): 29-44.

Hallegatte, Stéphanie. "Strategies to adapt to an uncertain climate change." Global Environmental Change 19 (2009): 240–47.

Harris, Shane. "Water Wars." Foreign Policy, September 18, 2014.

Hartmann, Betsy. "Rethinking Climate Refugees and Climate Conflict: Rhetoric, Reality and the Politics of Policy Discourse." Journal of International Development 22, no. 2 (2010): 233–46.

Hong, G., McLaren, J., 2014. Are Immigrants a Shot in the Arm for the Local Economy? National Bureau of Economic Research.

Holland, Andrew, and Xander Vagg. "The Global Security Defense Index on Climate Change." Washington, DC: American Security Project, 2013.

Homer-Dixon, Thomas F. Environment, Scarcity, and Violence. Princeton, NJ: Princeton University Press, 1999.

Hooghe, Liesbet, and Gary Marks. "Unraveling the Central State, but How? Types of Multi- level Governance." American Political Science Review 97, no. 2 (May 2003): 233–43.

Helsinki Process on Globalization and Democracy (2005, "Mobilizing Resources for the Millennium Development Goals", Report of the Track on the "Global Economic Agenda", Helsinki: Finnish Ministry for Foreign

Affairs.

Huddleston, T., 2016. Largest-ever European survey of immigrants gives big picture on long-term integration. Migration Policy Group.

Huntjens, Patrick. "Water management and water governance in a changing climate: Experience and insights on climate change adaptation in Europe, Africa, Asia and Australia." Eburon Academic Publishers, 2010.

Huntjens, Patrick, Claudia Pahl-Wostl, Benoit Rihoux, Maja Schlüter, Zsuzsanna Flachner, Susana Neto, Romana Koskova, Chris Dickens, and Isah Nabide Kiti, "Adaptive Water Management and Policy Learning in a Changing Climate: A Formal Comparative Analysis of Eight Water Management Regimes in Europe, Asia, and Africa," Environmental Policy and Governance 21, no. 3 (2011): 145–63.

Huntjens, Patrick, Louis Lebel, Claudia Pahl-Wostl, Jeff Camkin, Roland Schulze, and Nicole Kranz. "Institutional design propositions for the governance of adaptation to climate change in the water sector." Global Environmental Change 22, no. 1 (2012): 67–81.

Huysmans, Jef. The Politics of Insecurity: Fear, Migration and Asylum in the EU. Abingdon: Routledge, 2006.

Hoekman, Bernard. 2002. Economic development and the WTO after Doha. World Bank Policy Research Working Study 2851.

International Peace Institute, SDG Fund and Concordia, September 2017, Vienna, Austria; A New Way of Doing Business: Partnering for Peace and Sustainable Development.

Internal Displacement Monitoring Centre (IDMC). "Global Estimates: People Displaced by Disasters." Geneva: IDMC, September 2014.

International Crisis Group (ICG). "Water Pressure in Central Asia." Europe and Central Asia Report no. 233. Brussels: International Crisis Group, September 11, 2014.

Intergovernmental Panel on Climate Change (IPCC). Climate Change 2013: The Physical Science Basis. Working Group I, 5th Assessment Report. Cambridge: Cambridge University Press, 2013.

—. 1999. International liberalism and distributive justice: A survey of recent thought. World Politics 51(2): 269–96.

Ikenberry, G. John. 2001. After victory: Institutions, strategic restraint, and the rebuilding of order after major wars. Princeton: Princeton University Press.

International Labor Organization. 2004. A fair globalization: Creating opportunities for all. Geneva: Inter- National Labor Office.

John English, Ramesh Thakur, and Andrew F. Cooper (2005), a Leaders 20 Summit: Why, How, Who and When?, Waterloo: Centre for International Governance Innovation.

Juzwiak, T., McGregor, E., Siegel, M., 2014. Migrant and Refugee Integration in Global Cities: The Role of Cities and Businesses. The Hague Process on Refugees and Migration and UNU-MERIT & its School of Governance.

Krueger, Anne O. 1998. Whither the World Bank and the IMF? Journal of Economic Literature 36 (4): 1983–2020.

Kuper, Andrews. 2004. Democracy beyond borders: Justice and representation in global institutions. New York: Oxford University Press.

Kaufman, Robert R., and Alex Segura-Ubiergo. 2001. Globalization, domestic politics, and social spending in Latin America: A time-series cross-section analysis, 1973–97. World Politics 53 (4): 553–87.

Kelsen, Hans. Essays in Legal and Moral Philosophy. Translated by Peter Heath. Dordrecht: D. Reidel, 1973.

Korab-Karpowicz, W. Julian. “Political Realism in International Relations.” In The Stanford Encyclopedia of Philosophy, edited by Edward N. Zalta. Summer 2013 edition. Accessed 8 October 2014.

Kumm, Matthias. “The Cosmopolitan Turn in Constitutionalism: An Integrated Conception of Public Law.” Indiana Journal of Global Legal Studies 20 (2013): 605-628.

Keohane, Robert O. 1984. After hegemony: Cooperation and discord in the world political economy. Princeton: Princeton University Press.

Kemal Dervis (2005), a Better Globalization: Legitimacy, Governance and Reform, Washington: Center for Global Development.

Keil, Kathrin. “The Arctic: A New Region of Conflict? The Case of Oil and Gas.” Cooperation and Conflict 49, no. 2 (2014): 162–90.

Kelley, Colin P., Shahrzad Mohtadib, Mark A. Çanec, Richard Seagerc, and Yochanan Kushnirc. “Climate Change in the Fertile Crescent and Implications of the Recent Syrian Drought.” Proceedings of the National Academy of Sciences 112, no. 11 (2015): 3241–46.

Klaver, J., Odé, A., 2012. Civic integration in the Netherlands: a new approach towards citizenship, in: Cross-Border Welfare State: Immigration, Social Security and Integration. pp. 155–174.

Kochan, T., Bezrukova, K., Ely, R., Jackson, S., Joshi, A., Jehn, K., Leonard, J., Levine, D., Thomas, D., 2003. The effects of diversity on business performance: Report of the diversity research network. Hum. Resour. Manage. 42, 3–21.

Lazarova, M., Tarique, I., 2005. Knowledge transfer upon repatriation. J. World Bus. 40, 361–373.

Lucarelli, Sonia. “Introduction: Values, principles, identity and European Union foreign policy.” In Values and Principles in European Union Foreign Policy, edited by Sonia Lucarelli and Ian Manners, 1-18. London: Routledge, 2006.

Lukes, Steven. Power: A Radical View. Second edition. Houndmills: Palgrave Macmillan, 2004.

Legrain, P., 2016. Refugees Work: A Humanitarian Investment That Yields Economic Dividends. Tent Foundation and Open Political Economy Network. ManpowerGroup, 2016. 2016/2017 Talent Shortage Survey.

Lake, David. “Rightful Rules: Authority, Order, and the Foundations of Global Governance.” International Studies Quarterly 54 (2010): 587–613.

Larik, Joris. “Shaping the international order as an EU objective.” In The European Union’s Shaping of the International Legal Order, edited by Fabian Amtenbrink and Dimitry Kochenov, 62-86. Cambridge: Cambridge University Press, 2013.

Lebel, Louis, and B. T. Sinh. “Politics of floods and disasters.” In Democratizing Water Governance in the Mekong Region, ed. Louis Lebel,

J. Dore, R. Daniel, and Y. S. Koma, 37–54. Chiang Mai: Mekong Press, 2007.

"Legitimacy and Authority in International Politics." International Organization 53 (1999): 379-408.

Lebel, Louis, Tira Foran, Po Garden, and Jesse B. Manuta. "Adaptation to Climate Change and Social Justice: Challenges for Flood and Disaster Management in Thailand." In Climate Change Adaptation in the Water Sector, ed. Fulco Ludwig, Pavel Kabat, Henk van Schaik, and Michael van der Valk, 125–41. London: Earthscan, 2009.

Loser, Claudio M. 2004. External debt sustainability: Guidelines for low- and middle-income countries. G-24 Discussion Study Series 26. Geneva.

Lumsdaine, David Halloran. 1993. Moral vision in international politics: The foreign aid regime, 1949– 1989. Princeton: Princeton University Press.

Martin, Susan F. "Climate Change, Migration, and Adaptation." Study prepared for the Transatlantic Study Team on Climate-Induced Migration. Washington, DC: German Marshall Fund of the United States, June 2010.

Macedo, Stephen. 2004. What self-governing peoples owe to one another: Universalism, diversity and the law of peoples? Fordham Law Review 72 (5): 1721–38.

Mansfield, Edward D., Helen V. Milner, and B. Peter Rosendorff. 2002. Why democracies cooperate more: Electoral control and international trade agreements. International Organization 56 (3): 477–514.

Martin, Lisa, and Beth Simmons. 1998. Theories and empirical studies of international institutions. International Organization 52 (4): 729–57.

Mattoo, Aaditya, and Arvind Subramanian. 2004. The WTO and the poorest countries: The stark reality. IMF Working Study 04/81.

McGillivray, Fiona, and Alastair Smith. 2000. Trust and cooperation through agent specific punishments. International Organization 54 (4): 809–24.

McKinlay, Robert D, and Richard Little. 1977. A foreign policy model of US bilateral aid allocation. World Politics 30 (1): 58–86.

Maizels, Alfred, and Machiko K. Nissanke. 1984. Motivations for aid to developing countries. World Development 12 (9): 879–900.

Matthew, Richard. “Integrating Climate Change into Peace building.”Climatic Change 123, no. 1 (2014): 83–93.

Martin Albrow (1997), the Global Age: State and Society beyond Modernity, Stanford: Stanford University Press.

Martin Albrow (1999), Sociology: The Basics, London: Routledge, especially chapter 5, “Society in the Future”, pp. 141-169.

Martin, Susan F. “Climate Change, Migration, and Adaptation.” Study prepared for the Transatlantic Study Team on Climate-Induced Migration. Washington, DC: German Marshall Fund of the United States, June 2010.

Marimuthu, M., Arokiasamy, L., Ismail, M., 2009. Human capital development and its impact on firm performance: Evidence from developmental economics. J. Int. Soc. Res. 2, 265–272.

Martín, I., Arcarons, A., Aumüller, J., Bevelander, P., Emilsson, H., Kalantaryan, S., MacIver, A., Mara, I., Scalettaris, G., Venturini, A., Vidovic, H., van der Welle, I., Windisch, M., Wolffberg, R., Zorlu, A., 2016. From Refugees to Workers: Mapping Labor-Market Integration Support Measures for Asylum Seekers and Refugees in EU Member States (Volume I: Comparative Analysis and Policy Findings). Migration Policy Centre (MPC) and Robert Schuman Centre for Advanced Studies of the European University Institute in Florence (EUI).

Martin, Lisa L., and Beth A. Simmons. “International Organizations and Institutions.” In The Oxford Handbook of International Relations, edited by Christian Reus-Smit and Duncal Snidal, 192-211. Oxford: Oxford University Press, 2010.

Moellendorf, Darrel and Thomas Pogge, editors. Global Justice: Seminal Essays. St Paul, MN: Paragon House Publishers 2008.

Moravcsik, Andrew. “The New Liberalism.” in the Oxford Handbook of International Relations. In The Oxford Handbook of International Relations, edited by Christian Reus-Smit and Duncal Snidal, 234-254. Oxford: Oxford University Press, 2010.

McDonald, Matt. “Discourses of Climate Security.” Political Geography 33, no. 1 (2013): 42–51.

Manners, Ian. "Normative Power Europe: A Contradiction in Terms?" Journal of Common Market Studies 40 (2002): 235-258.

Meltzer, Alan. 2000. Report of the international financial institutions advisory commission. Meltzer Commission. Washington, DC.

Milner, Helen V. 1998. Rationalizing politics: The emerging synthesis of international, American, and comparative politics. International Organization 52 (4): 759–86.

Milner, Helen V., with Keiko Kubota. 2005. Why the move to free trade? Democracy and trade policy in the developing countries, 1970–1999. International Organization 59 (1): 107–43.

Milner, Helen V., B. Peter Rosendorff, and Edward Mansfield. 2004. International trade and domestic politics: The domestic sources of international trade agreements and organizations; The impact of international law on international cooperation. Eyal Benvenisti and Moshe Hirsch, eds. Cambridge UK, Cambridge University Press.

Mosley, Layna. 2003. Global capital and national governments. New York: Cambridge University Press.

Nagel, Thomas. 2005. The problem of global justice. Philosophy and Public Affairs. 33 (2): 113–47.

NBER macroeconomics annual 2000. Ben S. Bernancke and Kenneth Rogoff. Cambridge MA: MIT Press for NBER: 261–325.

Özden, Çaglar, and Eric Reinhardt. 2002. The perversity of preferences: GSP and developing countries trade policies, 1976–2000. World Bank Working Studies 2955.

Özden, Çaglar, and Eric Reinhardt. 2004. First do no harm: The effect of trade preferences on developing country exports. World Bank Research study.

Ortega, Martin. Building the future: The EU's contribution to global governance, EUISS Chaillot Study No. 100 (April 2007).

Oates, Wallace E. "Environmental Policy in the European Community: Harmonization or National Standards?" Empirica 25, no. 1 (1998): 1–13.

Oels, Angela. “From ‘Securitization of Climate Change to ‘Climatization’ of the Security Field: Comparing Three Theoretical Perspectives.” In Climate Change, Human Security and Violent Conflict, ed. Jürgen Scheffran, Michael Brzoska, Hans Günter Brauch, Peter Michael Link, and Janpeter Schilling. Heidelberg: Springer, 2012.

Ostrom, Elinor. “A Diagnostic Approach for Going beyond Panaceas.” Proceedings of the National Academy of Sciences 104, no. 39 (2007): 15181–87.

OECD, 2015. International Migration Outlook 2015. OECD Publishing, Paris.

OECD, 2012. Harnessing the skills of migrants and Diasporas to foster development: policy options. French Ministry of Foreign Affairs.

OECD (Ed.), 2010. Open for business: migrant entrepreneurship in OECD countries. OECD, Paris.

OECD/European Union, 2014. Matching Economic Migration with Labor Market Needs. OECD Publishing.

Peter, Fabienne. “Political Legitimacy.” In The Stanford Encyclopedia of Philosophy, edited by Edward N. Zalta. Spring 2014 edition. Accessed 8 October 2014.

Palmer, Margaret A., Catherine R. Liermann, Christer Nilsson, Martina Florke, Joseph Alcamo, P. S. Lake, and Nick Bond. “Climate change and the world’s river basins: Anticipating management options.” Frontiers in Ecology and Environment 6, no. 1 (2008): 81–89.

Pacific Institute. “The Water Conflict Chronology and Database.” The Pacific Institute, 2015.

Pogge, Thomas W. 2002. World poverty and human rights. Cambridge, UK: Polity.

Pogge, Thomans, and Sanjay Reddy. 2005. How *not* to count the poor. Forthcoming in Measuring global poverty, Sudhir Anand and Joseph Stiglitz, eds. Oxford: Oxford University Press.

Pritchett, Lant. 1997. Divergence, big time. Journal of Economic Perspectives 11 (3): 3–17.

Penninx, R., 2009. Decentralizing integration policies: Managing migration in cities, regions and localities, Policy Network.

Prime, J., Salib, E. R., 2014. Inclusive Leadership: The view from six countries. Catalyst. 16).

Public-Private Partnership in Infrastructure Resource Center, 2015. What are Public Private Partnerships? Public private partnership, World Bank Group. URL partnerships.

Peter B. Kenen, Jeffrey R. Shafer, Nigel L. Wicks, and Charles Wyplosz (2004), International Economic and Financial Cooperation: New Issues, New Actors, And New Responses, Geneva: International Center for Monetary and Banking Studies (ICMB) and Centre for Economic Policy Research (CEPR).

Prime, J., Salib, E. R., 2014. Catalyst on Inclusive Leadership: The view from six countries.

Public-Private Partnership in Infrastructure Resource Center, 2015. What are Public Private Partnerships? Public private partnership, World Bank Group. d 11.19.16).

Reed, H., Latorre, M., 2009. The economic impacts of migration on the UK labor market. Econ. Migr. Work. Pap. 3.

Reitz, J.G., 2001. Immigrant skill utilization in the Canadian labor market: Implications of human capital research. J. Int. Migr. IntegrationRevue Integr. Migr. Int. 2, 347–378.

Reed, H., Latorre, M., 2009. The economic impacts of migration on the UK labor market. Econ. Migr. Work. Pap. 3.

Reitz, J.G., 2001. Immigrant skill utilization in the Canadian labor market: Implications of human capital research. J. Int. Migr. Integration Revue Integr. Migr. Int. 2, 347–378.

Ruhs, M., Vargas-Silva, C., 2015. The Labor Market Effects of Immigration. Migration Observatory briefing, COMPAS, University of Oxford, UK.

"Role-identity and the Europeanisation of foreign policy: a political-cultural approach." In Rethinking European Foreign Policy, edited by Ben Tonra and Thomas Christiansen, 81-98. Manchester: Manchester

University Press, 2004.

Robert O. Keohane (2005), "The Contingent Legitimacy of UN-Based Multilateralism", prepared for a conference on "Legitimacy and Power in the Post-9/11 World" at the University of Southern California, Stanford Center for Advanced Study in Behavioral Sciences study dated April 5, 2005.

Ruhs, M., Vargas-Silva, C., 2015. The Labor Market Effects of Immigration. Migration Observatory briefing, COMPAS, University of Oxford, UK.

Ratner, Steven. "Ethics and international law: integrating the global justice project(s)." International Theory 5 (2013): 1-34.

Raz, Joseph. "On the Authority and Interpretation of Constitutions: Some Preliminaries." In Constitutionalism: Philosophical Foundations, edited by Larry Alexander, 152-193. Cambridge: Cambridge University Press, 1998.

Risse, Matthias. On Global Justice. Princeton, NJ: Princeton University Press, 2012.

Rodrik, Dani, Arvind Subramanian, and Francesco Trebbi. 2002. Institutions rule: The primacy of institutions over geography and integration in economic development. National Bureau of Economic Research Working Study 9305.

Romalis, John. 2003. Would rich country trade preferences help poor countries grow? Evidence from the generalized system of preferences, Manuscript.

Rose, Andrew K. 2002. Do WTO members have a more liberal trade policy? National Bureau of Economic Research Working Study 9347.

Rawls, John. 1999. The law of peoples; with, the idea of public reason revisited. Cambridge: Harvard University Press.

Risse, Mathias. 2004a. Does the global order harm the poor? Unpublished manuscript, Harvard University, John F. Kennedy School of Government.

Rodriguez, Francisco, and Dani Rodrik. 2001. Trade policy and economic growth: A skeptic's guide to the cross-national evidence.

Rodrik, Dani. 1996. Why is there multilateral lending? In Annual World Bank conference on development economics, 1995, ed. Michael Bruno and Boris Plees-kovic, 167–93. Washington, DC: International Monetary Fund.

Sayne, Aaron. Climate Change Adaptation and Conflict in Nigeria. Washington: United States Institute of Peace, June 2011.

Scheffran, Jürgen, Michael Brzoska, Hans Günter Brauch, Peter Michael Link, and Janpeter Schilling. Climate Change, Human Security and Violent Conflict. Heidelberg: Springer, 2012

Scheffran, Jürgen, Tobias Ide, and Janpeter Schilling. "Violent Climate or Climate of Violence? Concepts and Relations with Focus on Kenya and Sudan." International Journal of Human Rights 18, no. 3 (2014): 369–90.

Secretary General of the United Nations (2005), "In Larger Freedom: Towards Development, Security and Human Rights for All", Integrated and coordinated implementation of and follow-up to the outcomes of the major United Nations conferences and summits in the economic, social and related fields, United Nations: A/59/2005, 21 March 2005.

Stern, Nicholas. "The Structure of Economic Modeling of the Potential Impacts of Climate Change: Grafting Gross Underestimation of Risk onto Already Narrow Science Models." Journal of Economic Literature 51, no. 3 (2013): 838–59.

Sustainability and Equity: A Better Future for All. Human Development Report 2011. New York: Palgrave Macmillan, 2011.

Sachs, Jeffrey, and Andrew Warner. 1995. Economic reform and the process of global integration. Brookings Studies on Economic Activity (1): 1–118.

Sala-i-Martin, Xavier. 2002a. The world distribution of income (estimated from individual country distributions). NBER working study #8933.

—. 2002b. The disturbing "rise" of global income inequality. NBER Working Study 8904.

Schraeder, Peter J., Stephen W. Hook, and Bruce Taylor. 1998. Clarifying the foreign aid puzzle: A comparison of American, Japanese, French and Swedish aid flows. World Politics 50 (2): 294–323.

Sen, Amartya. 2000. Development as freedom. New York: Alfred A. Knopf.

Singer, Peter. 1972. Famine, affluence, and morality. Philosophy & Public Affairs 1 (3): 229–243.

Tänzler, Dennis, Alexander Carius, and Achim Maas. The Need for Conflict-Sensitive Adaptation to Climate Change. Berlin: Adelphi, 2013.

THP, 2014. Engagement with the Private Sector on International Migration: Mapping Study. The Hague Process on Refugees and Migration, Global Forum on Migration & Development, and the International Organization of Employers.

THP, 2015. The Return on Investment on Migration: What is in it for Business? The Hague Process on Refugees and Migration, The Hague.

THP, 2015. The Return on Investment on Migration: What is in it for Business? The Hague Process on Refugees and Migration, The Hague.

THP, 2014. Engagement with the Private Sector on International Migration: Mapping Study. The Hague Process on Refugees and Migration, Global Forum on Migration & Development, and the International Organization of Employers.

The Institutional Dimensions of Environmental Change: Fit, Interplay, and Scale. Global Environmental Accords: Strategies for Sustainability. Cambridge, MA: MIT Press, 2002.

The Role of International Organizations in the Global Economic Governance, Sterian Maria Gabriela, Romania Economic and Business Review, Special Issue, 2013

Trombetta, Maria J. "Climate Change and the Environmental Conflict Discourse." In Climate Change, Human Security and Violent Conflict, ed. Jürgen Scheffran, Michael Brzoska, Hans Günter Brauch, Peter Michael Link, and Janpeter Schilling. Heidelberg: Springer, 2012.

Trombetta, Maria J. "Linking climate-induced migration and security within the EU: Insights from the securitization debate." Critical Studies on Security 2, no. 2 (2014): 131–47.

UNHCR, 2016. Global Trends: Forced displacement in 2015. United Nations High Commissioner for Refugees.

United Nations, Department of Economic Affairs, Population Division, 2015. Trends in International Migrant Stock: The 2015 revision. United Nations database, POP/DB/MIG/Stock/Rev.2015.

United Nations General Assembly, 2013. Declaration of the High-level Dialogue on International Migration and Development (No. A/68/L.5). Draft resolution submitted by the President of the General Assembly.

United Nations (2004), A More Secure World: Our Shared Responsibility, Report of the Secretary-General's High-level Panel on Threats, Challenges and Change, United Nations.

United Nations Development Programme (UNDP). New Dimensions of Human Security. New York: Oxford University Press, 1994.

United Nations Environment Programme (UNEP). "From Conflict to Peace building: The Role of Natural Resources and the Environment." Nairobi: UNEP, 2009.

U.S. Agency for International Development (USAID). "Technical Publications on Conflict Management and Mitigation," 2015.

UNHCR, 2016. Global Trends: Forced displacement in 2015. United Nations High Commissioner for Refugees.

United Nations, Department of Economic Affairs, Population Division, 2015. Trends in International Migrant Stock: The 2015 revision. United Nations database, POP/DB/MIG/Stock/Rev.2015.

United Nations General Assembly, 2013. Declaration of the High-level Dialogue on International Migration and Development (No. A/68/L.5). Draft resolution submitted by the President of the General Assembly.

Wæver, Ole. "Securitization and Desecuritization." In On Security, ed. Ronnie Lipschut, 46–88. New York: Columbia University Press, 1995.

Wegge, Njord. "The Political Order in the Arctic: Power Structures, Regimes and Influence." Polar Record 47, no. 2 (2011): 1–12.

What's In Blue. "Arria Formula Meeting on Climate Change." February 14, 2013.

Wijnen, Marcus, Benedicte Augeard, Bradley Hiller, Christopher Ward, and Patrick Huntjens. "Managing the Invisible: Understanding and

Improving Groundwater Governance." Washington, DC: World Bank, Water Partnership Program, 2012.

WEF, 2014. Matching Skills and Labor Market Needs. Building Social Partnerships for Better Skills and Better Jobs, Global Agenda Council on Employment. World Economic Forum, Davos-Klosters, Switzerland 22-25 January.

WEF, 2013. The Business Case for Migration, The Network of Global Agenda Councils. World Economic Forum.

WEF, 2014. Matching Skills and Labor Market Needs. Building Social Partnerships for Better Skills and Better Jobs, Global Agenda Council on Employment. World Economic Forum, Davos-Klosters, Switzerland 22-25 January.

WEF, 2013. The Business Case for Migration, The Network of Global Agenda Councils. World Economic Forum.

—. 2000. Rawls's law of peoples. Ethics 110(4): 669–696.

—. 2005. Cosmopolitanism and global justice. The Journal of Ethics 9 (1–2): 11–27.

—. 2001b. The lost decades: Developing countries' stagnation in spite of policy reform, 1980–1998. Journal of Economic Growth 6 (2): 135–57.

—. 2003. Can foreign aid buy growth? Journal of Economic Perspectives 17 (3): 23–48.

—1978. A foreign policy model of the distribution of British bilateral aid, 1960–70. British Journal of Political Science 8 (3): 313–31.

—. 2004b. What we owe to the global poor. Journal of Ethics 9 (1/2): 81–117.

—. 1997. Has globalization gone too far? Washington, DC: Institute for International Economics.

—. 2000. Development strategies for the next century. Study prepared for the conference on "Developing Economies in the Twenty-First Century", Ciba, Japan, January 26–27.

—. 2004. Do we really know that the WTO increases trade? American Economic Review 94(1): 98–114.

—. 2002. One world: The ethics of globalization. New Haven: Yale University Press.

Samaha, Adam. "Dead Hand Arguments and Constitutional Interpretation." Columbia Law Review 108 (2008): 606-680

Scharpf, Fritz. Governing in Europe. Effective and Democratic? Oxford: Oxford University Press, 1999.

Schuman, Frederick L. International Politics: The Western State System in Transition. Third edition. London: McGraw-Hill, 1941.

Steinberg, Richard. 2002. In the shadow of law or power? Consensus-based bargaining and outcomes in the in the GATT/WTO. International Organization 56 (2): 339–74.

Stiglitz, Joseph E. 2002. Globalization and its discontents New York, NY: W. W. Norton.

Stone, Randall W. 2002. Lending credibility: The International Montetary Fund and the post-communist transition. Princeton: Princeton University Press.

Sinclair, Adriana. International Relations Theory and International Law. Cambridge: Cambridge University Press, 2010.

Subramanian, Arvind, and Shang-Jin Wei. 2003. The WTO promotes trade, strongly but unevenly. National Bureau of Economic Research Working Study 10024.

"The normative ethics of the European Union." International Affairs 84 (2008): 45- 60.

Tetlock, Philip E., and Aaron Belkin, eds. 1996. Counterfactual thought experiments in world politics: Logical, methodological, and psychological perspectives. Prince- ton: Princeton University Press.

Thacker, Strom Cronan. 1999. The high politics of IMF lending. World Politics 52 (1): 38–75.

"The Cosmopolitan Turn in Constitutionalism: On the Relationship between Constitutionalism in and beyond the State." In Ruling the World? International Law, Global Governance, Constitutionalism, edited by Jeffrey. L. Dunoff and Joel P. Trachtman, 258-326. Cambridge: Cambridge University Press, 2009.

United Nations Conference on Trade and Development (UNCTAD). 2004. Trade and poverty. Geneva: UNCTAD.

UNDP. 2004. Human development report 2004. New York: UNDP.

Van de Walle, Nicolas. 2001. African economies and the politics of permanent crisis, 1979–1999. New York: Cambridge University Press.

Vaubel, Roland. 1986. A public choice approach to international organization. Public Choice 51 (1): 39–57.

—. 1996. Bureaucracy at the IMF and the World Bank: A comparison of the evidence. World Economy 19 (2): 195–210.

"Values in EU Foreign Policy." In Beyond the Established Legal Orders: Policy Interconnections between the EU and the Rest of the World, edited by Malcolm Evans and Panos Koutrakos, 275-315. Oxford: Hart Publishing, 2011.

Vreeland, James Raymond. 2003. The IMF and economic development. New York: Cambridge University.

World Bank. 2002. World development indicators. Washington, DC: World Bank.

—. 2003. Annual report 2003. Washington, DC: World Bank.

—. 2004. Annual report 2004. Washington, DC: World Bank.

—. 2004. Global economic prospects. Washington, DC: World Bank.

World Trade Organization. 2003. World trade report 2003. Geneva: World Trade Organization.

—. 2004. International trade statistics. Geneva: World Trade Organization. (2011): 524-541.

Young, Oran R. Creating Regimes: Arctic Accords and International Governance. Ithaca, NY: Cornell University Press, 1998.

Zhang, Ting. "A Conflict-Sensitive Approach to Climate Change Mitigation and Adaptation in the Urbanizing Asia-Pacific." Working Study No. 7, The Hague Institute for Global Justice, 2015.

Zorlu, A., Hartog, J., 2001. Migration and Immigrants: The Case of the Netherlands (No. T1 2001-042/3), Tinbergen Institute Discussion Study. Tinbergen Institute and University of Amsterdam, Study prepared for Migration policy and the economy: international experiences, Munich: Hans Seidel Stiftung, 2001.

Zorlu, A., van der Welle, I., 2016. Case Study the Netherlands, in From Refugees to Workers: Mapping Labor-Market Integration Support Measures for Asylum Seekers and Refugees in EU Member States (Volume II: Literature Review and Country Case Studies). Migration Policy Centre (MPC) and Robert Schuman Centre for Advanced Studies of the European University Institute in Florence (EUI).